Carolyn Alexander

Bull Terriers

Everything About Purchase, Care,
Nutrition, Behavior, and Training

Filled with Full-color Photographs
Illustrations by Michele Earle-Bridges

BARRON'S

CONTENTS

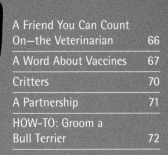

3

BULL TERRIER HISTORY

Known variously as the Clown of the Dog World, the White Cavalier, and the Canine Gladiator, the true identity of the Bull Terrier is rooted in its breed history. Key components to understanding the breed are based in an appreciation for the keen personable individuality of each Bull Terrier, their highly evolved intelligence, and the physical evolution that has brought us the dogs we love today.

Welcome to the world of the intelligent, personable Bull Terrier! Most are carefree clowns. Most are clever. Some are not—but every Bull Terrier is capable of making you smile.

Origins of the Breed

Although historians are not in agreement, Bull Terriers seem to have been in evidence as early as the 1500s in England. Writers in that era mentioned dogs that had physical and personality characteristics of dogs that were beginning to be called Bull and Terriers. Until the 1800s, very little was actually written about these dogs who were forerunners of Bull Terriers, and some of what was published must be viewed with

From tougher times, Bull Terriers were bred to be a gentleman's companion and they love family life and comfort.

some skepticism. For example, in the 1830s, writers in sporting magazines discussed such topics as the value of Bull Terriers bred from tall varieties of Scottish Terriers. We should perhaps assume that they were not referring to the rough-coated Scotties we know today.

The most concrete information that we have tells us that Bull Terriers are rooted in the English Bull Dog, which was very much dissimilar to the Bull Dog we know today. That Bull Dog was rather large, coarse, muscular, and roughly Mastiff-like. It had been developed in those tough times, when bull, badger, and bear baiting were considered sports. Major Count V. C. Hollender in his *The Bull Terrier and All About It* (circa 1934) states his belief that the Bull Terrier derived from breeding Fox Hounds, Mastiffs, Dalmatians, White Collies, Greyhounds, and Whippets, as well as Bull Dogs and White English Terriers. Writer Lt. Col. R. H. Glyn

A sturdy, proud Bull Terrier. The breed originated in the United Kingdom.

English Terrier, a breed that is unknown today and has been extinct for some time. These breedings provided an affable companion that maintained much of the Bull Dog's robust and hearty physique in a smaller size. Others bred the Bull Dog with the Black and Tan Terrier (also generally unknown today, but most tended to resemble large Manchester Terriers) to produce a compact dog of strength and tenacity who would perform in ratting pits. These dogs were also intelligent and seemed able to think and make immediate strategic decisions.

The stylish, healthy Spanish Pointer was used in many early English breeds and is also believed to have had some elemental role in early Bull and Terriers breedings, and Bull Terriers today are occasionally observed pointing. In those early days, no kennel club supervised the stud books or breeding records, and most of the information we have today is based on individuals who kept some records or at least wrote somewhat knowledgeably about breeds and occasionally about actual dogs that were bred.

Popularity: The Bull and Terrier enjoyed amazing popularity throughout most of the 1800s. Robert Leighton in his *Dogs and All About Them*, mentions that one was purchased at a very high price by Lord Camelford and given to a prize fighter. So notable was this that the dog was written about in the leading sporting magazines of the era. Leighton also explains that this breed, which was by the middle of that century mostly Terrier and perhaps only about 25 percent Bull Dog, was also enormously popular with students and residents at Oxford and Cambridge.

also held that Greyhounds were used, as did James Dickey, who also believed that some Italian Greyhounds were experimentally used in breeding early Bull and Terriers.

Bull and Terriers

Early Bull and Terriers were developed to work during the day helping eliminate vermin from homes, barns, and fields, and some to fight at night to bring in betting money. Somewhat surprisingly perhaps, these versatile dogs were reliable and loving with family members, including children. They were generally not used as watchdogs or guard dogs, and were considered dependable with people. Some Bull Dogs and Bull and Terriers were crossed with the White

CH Rocky Tops Sundance Kid ROM, the top winning American Bull Terrier of all time!

Development of the Breed

Somewhere in the 1850 and 1860 time frame, James Hinks of Birmingham began to take an assertive role in bringing the Bull Terrier into recognition as a distinct and distinctive breed. While others participated in the development of the breed, James Hinks' extensive breeding and solid reputation in the dog world earned him the title "Father of the Bull Terrier." The key to Hinks and his son Fred's success was based on crossing Bull and Terriers with Dalmatians, producing white dogs that were muscular, alert, and considered extraordinarily attractive. These white dogs showed a certain grace, style, and soundness and seemed to be a new, exciting breed. The bowed legs and mongrel look had given way to a dog of rather refined, well-built appearance, while retaining a plucky, stalwart disposition.

English dog shows: The first English dog show was held in 1859, but only Pointers and Setters were exhibited. Hinks introduced the first Bull Terriers at the 1860 Birmingham show. Somewhat surprisingly, conformation showing truly appealed to many Bull Terrier owners. The Bull Terrier Club was formed in 1887. Membership grew in popularity and today this premier English club has members all over the world.

Early Appearance

The Bull Terriers of the late 1800s were fairly well constructed with a sturdy, compact body shape of some elegance and agility. Virtually all had good strength of head, neck, and body, and ears that were cropped. Initially, ears were closely cropped to protect dogs involved in fighting or ratting, but eventually the smaller, upright ears were accepted as desirable because they presented an alert, attractive appearance. In the meantime, serious rumblings were becoming louder and more persistent against ear cropping and tail docking. In 1872 the celebrated writer Idstone railed against what he felt were barbarically conducted amputation procedures. The English Kennel Club banned cropping around 1889, but it wasn't initially enforced. However, in 1895 the Kennel Club, led by President S. E. Shirley, who actually was a well-known Bull Terrier breeder, resolutely, effectively banned cropping. Challenged to produce the desired erect ear naturally, Bull Terrier breeders succeeded within a surprising and relatively short time.

Deafness: In addition to a slight drop in popularity while breeders developed the stand-up ear, the Bull Terrier's reputation was suffering from concerns about a high proportion of deafness in the breed. In 1949 Harding Cox in *Dogs of Today* noted that many believed that cropping accounted for much of the deafness in Bull Terriers, adding ". . . some held the rather far-fetched idea that *all entirely white dogs* are apt to be deaf, or partially so." The relationship was *not* at all far-fetched, but love for the pure white dog was so earnest that most seemed to want to believe that deafness was serendipitous.

Identified as a hereditary defect, the prevailing deafness was found to be a particular degeneration or lack of a passage in the cochlear duct and was recognized even then to be a Mendelian recessive. If affected dogs were not bred, the problem would disappear. While some simply ignored scientific evidence and bred deaf dogs anyway, the real problem was that a unilaterally deaf dog (deaf in one ear) was also a carrier, and

in those years, there were no conclusive tests to determine partial deafness.

Colored Dogs

To engineer a heartier, healthier Bull Terrier, some breeders began introducing colored Staffordshire Bull Terriers into their lines. Since colored Bull Terriers bred to white or even-colored bred to colored (except for solid-colored dogs) can produce white dogs, this was an important step in developing healthier Bull Terriers, while retaining the white variety. While still producing the desired white puppies, breeders' use of colored dogs added some protection against deafness and skin problems. Unfortunately, so much controversy surrounded the introduction of colored Bull Terriers that good breeders of coloreds were not given the positive credit they deserved. A strong prejudice was generally held against white Bull Terriers, who were bred from two colored parents, which we now know was unwarranted and unwise.

While many educated writers such as Theo Marples weighed in on the side of the colored variety, others such as Adair Dighton considered the showing and breeding of colored Bull Terriers as almost unthinkable. In his book *The Bull Terrier and All About It* (United Kingdom, 1919), Dighton called it ". . . a retrogression in the breed, and I can definitely see no good in it whatever. The craze will not last and once it is gone breeders of the future will be left with pedigrees that will be uncertain in regard to the colour of the dogs. Enough trouble is caused with the occasional markings that crop up when

The Bull Terrier was known as the "Gentleman's Companion" and the "White Cavalier."

Initially controversial, the colored
Bull Terrier is now accepted and loved
by owners and breeders.

breeding from an all-white strain, but when brindles are mixed up indiscriminately with the all-whites, the confusion it will cause will be dreadful, and years must elapse before the influx of colour can be again bred out." The brindles that Dighton so disliked were needed in the breed and the colored Bull Terrier was finally recognized by the English Kennel Club in 1933.

The Treasured Pet

The Bull and Terrier emerged from a history of affiliation with distasteful sports and partnership with lowly crooks and vagrants like Bill Sykes to become the treasured pet of families, writers, actors, the rich, and the not-so-rich. Bull Terriers were bred from a variety of worthy breeds, producing an intelligent dog of basically healthy, hearty constitution. Today, Bull Terriers are first and foremost companion dogs. Their personalities have breed traits in common, but they are as individual as human children, and like children, socialization and training are critical to their development and good behavior. Good breeders are working today to continue the evolution of this family dog possessed of sweet disposition and playful, happy temperament.

The Bull Terrier in America

British Bull Terriers traveled with their masters and mistresses and were exported to continental Europe, India, South Africa, the American continent, and to Australia, where they became immensely popular. American and Canadian enthusiasts were less in number, but

they were ardent and sometimes combative proponents of the breed.

Early Shows

In 1885 a brindle female named Nellie II was the first Bull Terrier to be American Kennel Club (AKC)-registered. In 1877, at the first Westminster show, a single class was held for Bull Terriers, with females competing in that class against males. In the ensuing years, the infancy of this new sport was obvious as six-week-old puppies competed against veteran dogs and later, sizes were used as class breakdowns. Dogs didn't always have to win or even compete at breed level to compete for Best in Show.

Kennel names were not used and most dogs were known by single names. Rarely were dams or sires listed and often no data on color or breeder was included in show information. In the 1890s Ch. Tommy Tickle, Ch. Princeton Monarch, and Ch. Woodcote Wonder were the top-winning Bull Terriers in this emerging and engaging pastime. The first Best in Show Bull Terrier is believed to be a white male known simply as "Count." The first Bull Terrier and the first Canadian dog to win Westminster Best in Show (BIS) was the white male Ch. Haymarket Faultless in 1918. He was 18 months old at the time. In 2006 the second Bull Terrier to win BIS at Westminster was the gorgeous, record-setting red smut Ch. Rocky Tops Sundance Kid ROM.

Natural companions for children, Bull Terriers are devoted to making life fun!

Cropping ban: In 1895, the American Kennel Club, aware of the English cropping ban, instigated debates on the topic. The AKC voted against a ban, but some delegates reprised the topic. Contemptuous of AKC efforts to ban cropping, the Bull Terrier Club of America (BTCA) Board publicly ridiculed AKC delegates and personnel who advocated the change. Since political retribution was not looked upon with favor by the AKC, the BTCA was condemned for intimidating and unseemly actions. The AKC, which at that time was made up of individual and club memberships, suspended the BTCA and BTCA members from AKC affiliation. This initially intense situation was resolved relatively amicably and surprisingly quickly. The BTCA filed a new application for AKC membership. In December 1897 the BTCA again became the Bull Terrier parent club in the United States and has remained so ever since. Controversy over ear cropping continued to subside as the naturally erect ear became more commonplace.

The Standard

The next storm that hit the BTCA came when the colored Bull Terrier was considered for admission to the AKC and was resolved in this country by recognition as one breed with two varieties. In the first decade of the twentieth century, there was considerable debate on how the standard should address head shape, overall type, and size. Ultimately, in 1915 the AKC published the standard for the "Bullterrier," later changed to read "Bull Terrier." The standard as revised in 1936 still referred to a cropped or uncropped ear, but the 1957 standard removed

Everywhere except the United States, colored and white Bull Terriers compete in the same ring. In the U.S., they are considered separate varieties of the same breed.

any reference to cropping. Other changes over the years had to do with weight, color, and faults. The current standard has been effective since 1974.

Varieties: What is critically different about the AKC standard versus those in other countries is that in the United States, colored and white Bull Terriers are considered different varieties of the same breed. They are not shown against each other in the same ring, with the sole exception that at independent specialties the top-winning colored may compete against the top-winning white. At group shows, both the Best of Variety (BOV) colored and the BOV white advance to show in the Terrier Group against other terriers. In all other countries of the world, including our neighbor Canada, colored and white compete against each other and only one proceeds to group level.

Separation of the varieties will likely never change as Americans enjoy the additional trophies and the lower point count required to finish championships. The Recognition of Merit (ROM) program, which was instituted by the BTCA at the behest of Robert Oppenheimer, acts as something of a methodology for equating American ROM champions with English champions.

A Breed with Pizzazz and Personality

The BTCA's relationship to the AKC initially was a rocky road that has smoothed considerably in the last half century. This progress is due in part to Bull Terrier owners taking more of a role in all-breed clubs and attending all-breed shows, and BTCA leadership in unifying and expanding Bull Terrier interests through regional breed clubs and in the AKC. Bull Terriers and their people are particularly fortunate to have the Honorable David Merriam watching over them. Active in breeding and exhibiting Bull Terriers from his youth, he advanced to considerable personal success as a California judge, an AKC Terrier Group judge, and a leader in the American Kennel Club. His guidance and statesmanship have been invaluable to the BTCA and its membership.

All breeds have members who are headstrong and decisively interesting characters. It seems that Bull Terrier people are often some of the most remarkable, colorful, and determined of dog folk—they are never dull! Bull Terrier people, like their dogs, love to have a good time and are willing to persevere for the result they want. Those who join the ranks of Bull Terrier owners and BTCA membership will rarely find life boring.

THE MODERN BULL TERRIER

The modern Bull Terrier has a delightful temperament, unique head, and strong body.

Known Breeders

Much of the progress of the contemporary Bull Terrier was accelerated by English influences led by Raymond Oppenheimer. Possessed of great wealth, position, and considerable power, Oppenheimer loved Bull Terriers and was determined to bring them into contemporary society and life. His reign in the Bull Terrier world ran remarkably from the 1940s until his death in 1984.

Other strong figures who participated in advancing Bull Terriers included Eva Weatherill, Gladys Adlam, and Violet Drummond Dick to name a few. We knew and had great respect for Violet, who bred Ch. Abraxas Audacity, the only Bull Terrier to win Best in Show at Crufts in England.

Bull Terriers have a keen and intelligent expression.

These breeders and many others of lesser fame, were working diligently to breed not only dogs of reliable temperament, but also dogs of considerable beauty and good health. Early standards had distinguished the Bull Terrier from other breeds, but in the late 1900s great progress was made in developing the unique egg-shaped head with the tiny, dark triangular eyes, which is the hallmark of the breed.

Screening and Breeding

Good breeders began screening and breeding only Bull Terriers who exhibited excellent sweet temperaments, good hearing, and the desirable curving profile. Developing the football head was in keeping with historical perspective that encouraged the long, elliptical, large-sized head as desirable. Early breeders who wanted real quality also sought to breed short-backed,

The Bull Terrier nose should be black with well-developed nostrils.

well-built dogs who moved with agility on straight fronts and well-angulated rears. They wanted to see a jaunty, spirited, medium-sized dog chasing squirrels and playing in the yard, sleeping on the couch, and winning at dog shows.

Head: The development of the egg-shaped head was encouraged principally by breeder judges who rewarded excellence in head type and shape. By 2000 some heads were actually becoming overdone, so much so that they appeared to be parrot-beaked, usually with a loss of lower jaw strength. Fortunately, good judges and breeders know that balance and overall quality, not a single attribute on its own, make for long-term success. Thoughtful breeders in these times are working to maintain beautiful heads on handsome, shapely bodies.

Most judges, whether breed specialists or not, are educated to look for that oval, filled-up head and short-backed, muscular, squarish body, jaunty movement, and happy spirit.

Today's Bull Terrier

The Bull Terrier has a curious persona that includes the occasional dance of joy, when he sprints about the house or yard in complete abandon and then suddenly stops and grins. Some call these maneuvers "Bully runs" and they are remarkable for their intensity, short duration, and lack of damage caused. Many will seem to lightly prance when a tablecloth or branch of a bush brushes their backs as they walk under it. The Bull Terrier is a dynamo and a darling. Most play like a tomboy one minute

A true Bull Terrier is fit and trim, well exercised, hail, hearty, and much loved!

and the next they are gathering up the softest pillows for a nap.

The Bull Terrier of this era has kept his sturdy fighting form, but replaced his combative nature with a delightful personality that is more comedian than gladiator. His completely unique head and compact body give a special silhouette that anyone should be able to recognize from a great distance. The ring warrior and gentlemen's companion of old is now a companion of idiosyncratic style, distinctive appearance, and eccentric charm. He is loved by those who appreciate his uniqueness and ability to add dimension and depth and joy to their lives.

The Bull Breeds Family

Generally, the "Bull Breeds" are considered to be Bull Terriers, Staffordshire Bull Terriers, American Staffordshire Terriers, Bull Mastiffs, Pit Bull Terriers, and American Bull Dogs. Of these, the first four are AKC-recognized breeds. All six are UKC-registered.

Differences Within the Family

Physically, the principal differences in breeds are in head shape and size. Bull Terriers and Staffordshires are the smallest of these breeds. The Bull Terriers' clownish nature and unique football-shaped head tend to differentiate

Dogs, like people, must be judged by their actions, not for the way they look.

them from the other Bull Breeds. The Bull Mastiff and American Bull Dog are classified as Working Breeds, while the other four are terriers. All of these breeds when well bred, properly trained and cared for are wonderful companions. Most are loyal guardians of their families and were bred over time to be fully responsive to and good-natured with people.

Breed Specific Legislation

Too often, Bull Breeds and sometimes Rottweilers, Mastiffs, and others are the targets of Breed Specific Legislation (BSL). BSL is a political solution that punishes dogs and their owners because of the way a dog looks, and tends to be based on an emotional response to a specific situation and ill-informed public hysteria, rather than being based on actual facts and valid data. Laws that discriminate based on

A plain, old-fashioned head on a well constructed ten-week-old puppy.

appearance are unfair and un-American. Law enforcement and animal control officials often cannot tell the difference between breeds. In one of the early Pit Bull frenzies, German Shepherd dogs and all manner of mixed breeds were misidentified as Pit Bulls. The Pit Bull label too often was and is meant to denigrate dogs without actual proof of bad behavior.

Carefully managed, lawful, fairly administered control of everyone who keeps and breeds dogs would reduce the number of dogs and cats dumped in shelters, and cut back on animal cruelty. All dogs should be microchipped or tattooed to provide accurate ownership records. If owners were held completely liable for injury or damage caused by their dogs and for care of dogs they have bred and own, many of our problems with mismanaged dogs and BSL would end. If people had to register each and every puppy, how many unwanted litters would continue to be born? Unfortunately, such careful control is contrary to long-established American practices and traditions. Band-aid legislation such as BSL tends to be applied, rather than real, workable solutions.

BSL is a sad commentary on a society that too quickly bases law on appearance, race, and color, rather than on reason and farsighted law that provides opportunity where responsibility is accepted. Law and punishment should be based on behavior, not on parentage, color, appearance, or breed.

BULLY STARS

In contemporary use, "star" often tends to mean a pop icon. In terms of Bull Terriers, we have several recent trendy icons such as the Target dog, who is actually a number of different Bull Terriers and sometimes Miniature Bull Terriers. Most are delighted in the interest shown to our breed by the Target Corporation, whose management generously donated to Bull Terrier Rescue in 2004. Target's "Bullseye" seems to be a positive and recognizable representative of our breed.

Famous Bull Terrier Owners

✔ Singer Rick Springfield's white Bull Terrier, Ronnie, has appeared on several album covers, which are now collectibles for fans of the singer as well as the dog.

✔ The famous, glamorous actress Delores Del Rio of the '30s and '40s owned a handsome white male named Ch. Faultless of Blighty.

✔ The celebrated British golfer Sir Henry Thomas Cotton, who three times won the British Open, owned a white male named Johnnie. Johnnie was a gift from Raymond Oppenheimer who chaired the Golf Foundation Committee upon which Sir Henry served as

Bull Terriers come in two varieties: colored and solid white.

a founding member. Known for his soft, sweet personality, Johnnie got along well with cats and loved to sleep with toys and dolls.

✔ Prominent hotelier Sir Harry Preston's best-known Bull Terrier was a white male named Sambo, who was reliably reported to have lived 17 years, most of that time at the Royal York Hotel in Brighton, England.

✔ The-long time London Zoo Superintendent, Dr. Geoffrey Vevers, owned a number of outstanding Bull Terriers from boyhood. He commissioned and presented the now-famous perpetual Regent Trophy to the English Bull Terrier Club.

✔ Every hockey fan and most Canadians instantly recognize Don Cherry and his celebrated Blue! The original Blue, a gift from his Bruins, died in 1989, but the revered and

Spuds

A predecessor icon of considerable fame was Spuds MacKenzie, whose sensational Budweiser marketing career began at the 1987 Super Bowl. While touted as something of a "babe magnet," Spuds was in reality a lovely female Bull Terrier whose real name was Ch. Honey Tree Evil Eye. We had the good fortune to meet "Spuds" in Los Angeles when she was in town for a commercial shoot. Her advertising career was cut relatively short by those who felt Spuds made beer drinking too appealing for young people; nonetheless, Spuds is still regarded by most with great fondness.

controversial Cherry always has a white Bull Terrier named Blue with him on book and album covers, on beer kegs, and in his home.

Bully Literary Stars

• One of the most famous dogs of the early 1900s was actually only partly Bull Terrier. Dreadfully abused by his original owner, Joe was rescued by a good-hearted woman named Louise Moore. Margaret Marshall Saunders stayed with the Moore family for a time and felt that Joe's story was important. In 1893 Saunders submitted *Beautiful Joe* in a writing contest, omitting her obviously female first name. Narrating the tale of his experiences from the dog's point of view was unusual and brilliantly effective. Published in 1894, it was the first Canadian book to sell over one million copies and by 1930 sales exceeded seven million copies. The lesser-known sequel, *Beautiful Joe's Paradise*, is also loved by Bull Terrier advocates.

• War correspondent, novelist, and playwright Richard Harding Davis seemingly never owned a Bull Terrier, but one of his most compelling and famous books was *Bar Sinister*, which was later the basis for the 1955 movie *It's a Dog's Life*. Published in 1905, *Bar Sinister* was a rags-to-riches or low-life-to-blue-ribbon tale that also effectively employed the Bull Terrier hero as the narrator.

• John Steinbeck's best-known canine companion was Charley, his poodle, but Steinbeck also had a white Bull Terrier, whom he loved passionately.

• Another accomplished author, James Thurber, occasionally wrote of his childhood pal, an American Bull Terrier named Rex. Many mistakenly believe the Bull Terrier was the basis for his story "The Dog Who Bit People." However, that honor rests with his rather notorious, personable, and much loved Airedale, Muggs.

• One of the great illustrators and painters of all time, Cecil Charles Windsor Aldin, made famous a charismatic Bull Terrier named Cracker. This fine artist captured the essence of Bull Terrier character and canine relationships in his wonderfully expressive drawings. Aldin's sketches of Cracker and his canine buddies, especially works with Micky, the Irish Wolfhound, are prized by animal and art lovers the world over.

• Celebrated Scottish writer, Sir Walter Scott's favorite dog was a Bull Terrier named Camp, whom he regarded as the smartest dog he'd ever known. Scott obtained Camp about the time of his marriage and Camp was the couple's utterly biddable and constant companion for the next 11 years. So close was their relationship, that Camp was included in three early Scott portraits and at his death, Camp was

Reading about Bull Terriers will give you more insight into their friendly, courageous personalities. Your Bull Terrier would love to share that quiet reading time with you.

buried just outside his master's window, so he would never be far away.

• Sheila Burnford's *The Incredible Journey* was first published in London in 1961. Set in Canada, this prize-winning, enormously successful story was about a Bull Terrier, a Golden Retriever, and a Siamese cat trying to find their way home. Almost instantly, Bodger became the favored name for Bull Terriers. Disney made the book into a movie in 1963 and then remade it 30 years later, titling it *Homeward Bound* and giving the Bull Terrier's title role to an American Bull Dog.

• Famous for his wonderful children's books, most of which include a Bull Terrier, Chris Van Allburg's best-known Bull Terrier character is the mischievous Fritz from his *Garden of Abdul Gasazi*.

• Catherine Cookson included Bill the Bull Terrier in *Mary Ann and Bill*.

• Dodie Smith wrote about a fictional Bull Terrier, Heloise, in *I Capture the Castle*.

• Loren Spiotta-DiMare and Tom Chapin wrote a true and truly wonderful story about *Caesar: On Deaf Ears*.

• Canadian Marsha Boulton has written a number of brilliantly funny books about life in the country with her Bull Terrier, Wally the Wonder Dog.

• Collectors especially will enjoy Cowles' *Maera and His Master*, Sumerwell's *Four in the Family*, and Griffith's *Grip*. And there are actually two Westerns that include Bull Terriers: *Grace Harlowe's Overland Riders in the North Woods* and Max Brand's *The White Wolf*.

Cartoons: Some literary Bull Terriers aren't actual dogs at all. Best known for his New Yorker cartoons, George Booth was probably one of the most popular of twentieth century artists

spoken words of wisdom. Floyd is less a dog than he is an easygoing companion, who seems to truly enjoy his partnership with quirky, flippant Maxine.

In the Houses of State

Two American presidents have owned Bull Terriers. Theodore Roosevelt's Pete reportedly was protective and as energetic as his owner. Having something of a reputation, Pete was eventually banished from White House residency reportedly after taking a nip out of the posterior of the visiting French ambassador! Theodore's daughter Ethel for a short period had a white Bull Terrier named Mike, but he didn't get along with her horse, Fidelity.

A white male named Whitestock Service Man was the next Bull Terrier to live in the White House. President Woodrow Wilson called him Bruce. Unlike Pete or Mike, Bruce was known for his plucky, but gentle, sweet disposition.

Princess Margaret was a colorful, but hard-working British Royal; she had two white Bullies, Florence and Dotty, whose reputations were unfortunately a bit tarnished. The English press occasionally called the girls "Pit Bulls," presumably less out of ignorance than to subtly irritate the royal family.

Movies, Television, and Stage Stars

While some affectionately claim Petey from the *Our Gang* and *Little Rascals* comedies to be a Bull Terrier, he was one of the first Stafford-

to show the bizarre and funny side of a Bull Terrier. Of current fame, Grimmy is a character borne of the incredible artistry of Mike Peters, who has put this Bull Terrier star in best-selling comic strips and books. Peters seems to recognize the Bull Terrier's natural comedic personality and innate ability to get into the most ridiculous situations. While Grimmy is an exaggeration, he is loved the world over for his over-the-top sense of sly humor.

Another popular Bull Terrier cartoon character is of course Floyd of Hallmark's cranky, blue-haired Maxine fame. Created by John Wagner, the loyal Floyd plays empathetic straight man to Maxine's often outrageous and always out-

shire Terriers to be registered by the AKC. The 1955 film *It's a Dog's Life* was based loosely on Richard Harding Davis' book, *Bar Sinister*. The star was a white Bull Terrier named Wildfire, who had his own stunt double Bull Terrier. In the 1970 film *Patton*, George C. Scott shared the stage with a white Bull Terrier that portrayed Willie. Bull Terriers have been seen in a number of recent movies such as Damon Wayan's *Bulletproof*, and they have very occasionally been seen in television programs. A Miniature Bull Terrier starred in Disney's *Babe— Pig in the City*, but was mislabeled a Pit Bull. Meathead of *Baa Baa Black Sheep* television fame was alleged to have been Pappy Boyington's Bull Terrier. The short-lived, but entertaining, series in the 2002–2003 television season called *Keen Eddie* featured a Miniature Bull Terrier, Pete. In the movie and stage play *Oliver*, a Bull Terrier of course, played Bullseye.

Military Heroes

To their credit, several Pit Bulls and mixed-breed Bull Terriers served during the Civil War, World War I, and World War II. The most decorated American war dog, Stubby, was a beautiful Pit Bull, who most of us would like to think had some Bull Terrier blood in those courageous veins. Found at Yale University in 1917, Stubby served and was wounded in World War I, receiving multiple medals including one from General John J. Pershing.

A personable white Bull Terrier named Nelson served with Vice Admiral Gordon Campbell on the *H.M.S. Cumberland* from 1906 to 1919. His charming bio *Dog Nelson AB* was illustrated by Peter Fraser. A brindle Bull Terrier, Jake, served with Captain Edward Hazlett on the U.S. sub-

Bull Terriers served with American soldiers and sailors.

marine, the *Starfish*. A white male named Major served with a New Zealand regiment in the Mediterranean in 1940 until his death and burial in Italy in 1944 next to other officers from his unit.

The most famous of the Army boys, however, were probably General George S. Patton's Bull Terriers. Patton's first Bull Terrier, Tank, turned out to be completely deaf. Although purchased for Patton's daughters, Tank was closest to Patton. Tank enjoyed a full, happy life with the family despite his deafness. William the Conqueror, better known as Willie, joined the Patton household in 1944 and rarely left Patton's

A beautiful, well-trained Bull Terrier is a joy to live with and to show!

home and lived the balance of his natural life with the Patton family.

Truly Special Bull Terriers

In 1929 a Bull Terrier known as Peggy saved an English boy from drowning by swimming out and bringing him back to shore. Some Bull Terriers swim, while others seem to detest water and sink like bricks. The only known water life-saving Bull Terrier, Peggy is also reputed to have saved her family's home by barking when clothing next to an unattended fireplace caught fire.

Bull Terriers are known for their ability to survive and even triumph over incredible hardship. In 1929, a white Bull Terrier was born in Portland, Oregon. Sent to Juneau, Alaska, the puppy was abandoned when she was found to be stone deaf. Initially, she survived by scrounging food. Eventually named Patsy Ann, she began to be recognized for her stalwart, friendly patrolling of the wharf and enthusiastic greeting of ships. She had an unerring sense of when ships were coming and which docks would be their berths. Amazed residents began to welcome her to their businesses for treats and meals, but she did not stay with anyone; her home was the wharf. In 1934 the mayor of Juneau hailed her as the Official Greeter of Juneau. Patsy Ann died in March 1942. Fifty years later, well-known artist Anna Burke Harris' bronze statue of Patsy Ann was unveiled on the wharf to honor this friendly Bull Terrier's patient spirit and offer hospitable greeting to all visitors.

Even knowing these honorable predecessors, most will recognize that truly the most special Bull Terrier is the one lying at your feet as you are reading this!

side from the moment of his arrival. Willie was in a number of Patton photos, the most famous of which is the haunting photo of Willie lying next to Patton's trunk after Patton's untimely death. A friend who was the librarian at the Patton Library told me that the most frequently asked question of the staff was "What happened to Willie?" The answer is that Willie came

Most judges know the value of a solid brindle, even though they don't have flashy white markings.

FINDING THE RIGHT BREEDER AND PUPPY

Because you will live with this puppy for 9 to 14 years, depending mostly on your care and his genetics, you'll want to plan your search strategy carefully. Reading this book is a great start.

Research! Research! Research!

Contact the Bull Terrier Club of America (BTCA) or a local Bull Terrier club for a list of recommended breeders. The *www.BTCA.com* site offers referrals to the Web sites of most local clubs. Consider attending a meeting or club event to meet Bull Terriers and their people. Joining the club can also be a great way to get to know breeders and help you determine with whom you might like to work and whose puppies you'd probably be happiest having. Club members can also be helpful and supportive in later training, veterinarian referrals, and enjoyable Bull Terrier activities. Getting to know other Bull Terrier folks is part of the joy of the Bully experience.

Puppies love attention, so they love training. It just has to be fun!

Buyers should talk to different breeders and visit their homes. Are the adult dogs and puppies clean and well cared for? Do they look and act healthy? Ask to see the mother and observe her personality. Ask her age. Females are normally bred only between two and seven years of age. If the breeder has both mother and father on the premises, ask if this is a repeat breeding of the dam and sire and how many litters the dam has had previously. Most good breeders do not keep both dam and sire. It certainly happens, but it can be a warning sign. Unlike puppy millers, reputable breeders rarely repeat a breeding and most females are not bred more than three times in total.

Imported puppies: Be wary of litters of puppies imported from overseas and anyone who offers to deliver puppies. Buyers deserve to meet the mother of puppies and see where they were whelped and raised. Some good

Multiple Breeds

Be suspicious if the breeder sells more than one or perhaps two breeds of dogs; most good breeders specialize in only one or two breeds. Having more is very possibly indicative of a puppy mill.

breeders do import quality dogs and the occasional puppy, but many disreputable entrepreneurs are importing baby puppies from Russia, old Soviet bloc countries, and other places. Generally, buyers will never receive registration papers and the puppies they do receive are likely to be poor quality and prone to a variety of physical and mental problems. A puppy is an important investment and will be a family member. Be prepared to visit each and every breeder being considered.

Start your search for information and a good breeder at **www.BTCA.com**

Questions and Interviews

Don't just look for a cute face or grab the first puppy who comes to you. Expect the breeder to first talk over your lifestyle and expectations. Expect the breeder to talk about the parents, how to evaluate a puppy, how to pick up and hold a puppy, and the differences between the puppies' personalities. Breeders will explain details about their contracts and want to talk about training, socialization, and diet. The discussion with the breeder should include the health issues covered in the Healthy, Wealthy, and Wise chapter (page 53). Well-bred Bull Terriers should be healthy mentally and physically.

Buyers should ask questions about the health, virtues, and faults of the parents and grandparents of the puppy. Good breeders are happy to talk to prospective owners about the puppy's background and specific dogs in the pedigree. Most will be honest about good points and possible problems, and will show you credentials for AKC titles, Baer testing, and pedigrees. Most can show photos of canine relatives in the BTCA publications, *Barks* and *The Record*. Puppy millers boast, but rarely back up claims with real documentation.

Bull Terrier Clubs

Buyers should inquire about Bull Terrier clubs to which the breeder belongs. Good breeders are active in local Bull Terrier club(s) and the Bull Terrier Club of America. If a seller tends to sneer at club membership or the value of showing, a buyer should be suspicious of their commitment to the betterment of the breed.

Note: Be very wary of breeders who say they belong to "AKC." AKC members are clubs, not

Good breeders will document pedigrees, registration, and health records at or before the time of sale.

individuals; however, less than reputable breeders say this to mislead buyers.

Shows

Buyers should ask the breeder to discuss the personality of each puppy and discuss their lifestyle and expectations. Even if the puppy is not liable to be shown, buyers should ask the breeder to evaluate the puppy in terms of the AKC standard. This helps buyers understand what is important and tells them whether the breeder is really knowledgeable. Most good breeders show. Potential buyers should go to at least one show, where they watch and compare dogs and the people involved with them. This experience is especially valuable at specialties or matches, when larger numbers of Bull Terriers and breeders are present. Those interested in potential show puppies should make sure that they have gone to several shows, including

specialties, before making any purchase. Buyers who feel the least bit hesitant should ask for references. Good breeders can introduce you to others who have purchased from them or who co-own with them.

Caveats: If the breeder does not have AKC paperwork or offers puppies younger than eight weeks old or seems mostly interested in money and offers to let a buyer select *any* puppy, walking out should be seriously considered. If the puppy's AKC registration form is not available, buyers should assume that the puppy is not and will never be registered, and may *not* be purebred. A printed pedigree is not enough.

Thoughtful breeders: Potential buyers should also be prepared and patient, because thoughtful breeders interview carefully, often asking potential buyers to visit several times, and sometimes will ask to make a house check. This is all to help buyers find the puppy whose

personality best suits their family and situation. Because of their highly individual natures and activity levels, Bull Terrier puppies and families who are best suited to each other are more likely to successfully bond and be happy in the long term.

Many good breeders have waiting lists. Most don't advertise or ship. Buyers may need to be willing to travel to meet the breeder and puppy. Smart buyers welcome a breeder's interest and involvement. Good breeders make themselves available to help with answers and advice, and their friendship can be a very worthwhile part of the entire experience.

Buyers

Smart buyers are informed and realistic. They ask questions, understanding that when dealing with genetics, recessives can surface that even the best breeder could not predict. For their part, good breeders screen buyers and breeding animals to minimize problems and maximize the joy of a Bull Terrier ownership. Good communication is crucial to a long-term affiliation

with the breeder and others in the breed. Flexibility and complete honesty with your breeder are keys to finding the right Bull Terrier and resolving questions or problems as they occur. Buyers not opposed to showing should ask if the breeder will assist in helping them learn more about showing. Most will be pleased to help. Showing can be a delightful new way to grow, learn, and make new friends.

Buyers must examine their reasons for wanting this new family member, who will require time and training, who will need love and attention, and whose philosophy about laughter and comfort is unique and particularly engaging. Bull Terriers are not for everyone. They are not status symbols, collectible statues, or guard dogs, and they will not stay puppy-sized for very long. Most are bright and go quickly from cute baby to being an active family member. Bull Terriers are for special people willing to open their lives and hearts by committing to a long-term relationship with a playful child in a dog suit.

Buying, Owning, and Loving a Bull Terrier

Contracts and Co-ownership

Caring breeders want to continue to be involved with the puppy and the new owners, and will be readily available for questions. While many find the idea of co-ownership offensive, it is fairly common practice with better Bull Terrier breeders. Because of the strength and sensitive nature of the breed and because these breeders have spent countless hours studying pedigrees, analyzing phenotype, genotype, and health factors, they want to be sure that puppies go to homes where they will be well cared for and not be unwisely bred.

Contracts: Most good Bull Terrier breeders have contracts that specify if a puppy is to be shown or bred, pending health tests as an adult. Contacts will specify neutering if a puppy is not to be bred or shown. Rarely is the decision on whether a puppy is a show puppy or not, clear at nine weeks of age. Flexibility on the part of the buyer and breeder can be helpful, and appropriate options should be addressed in the contract. Buyers should carefully review and honestly discuss the contract with the breeder. Most breeders get along very well with their co-owners and are supportive of them. They are available for advice and to help the owner learn to show, how to fill out entries, about show etiquette, which shows to attend, locating training classes, decisions involved in breeding, and other important activities and decisions. A good breeder belongs to the BTCA and usually at least one regional Bull Terrier club, and will normally be willing to sponsor puppy owners' membership too. Co-ownership can be a valuable resource, especially for those interested in learning to show and those who have a serious long-term interest in the breed.

Price: Essentially, the puppy price includes this important assistance and advice. Buyers should naturally seek breeders who are reputable, rather

Visiting puppies and their mother in the breeder's home is an important part of acquiring a quality puppy.

—— T I P ——

Names

In most reputable pedigrees, dogs' names are prefaced with the breeder's kennel name. Most Bull Terriers' registered names are fun, unusual, multiple names that are not overly pretentious.

than simply buying from whoever has puppies when they are starting to look around. Buying a puppy tends to be an emotional decision, but mental clarity and diligence in finding a healthy puppy from a good breeder is far more important than immediate availability.

The Importance of Bonding

Most breeders place a puppy when they feel that the puppy is ready to venture from the

TIP

Tips for the Buyer

Ask about and review documentation for:
- Health and health testing of puppies, parents, and grandparents.
- Age of parents and puppies.

Discuss with the breeder:
- The personality and readiness level of each puppy being considered.
- How the standard applies to puppies being considered.
- The contract.

Don't buy a puppy if:
- There is no documentation of health testing for puppy or parents.
- The AKC individual registration form cannot be completed when the puppy goes home.

nest. Usually, this is at about eight weeks of age, but it may be a little later depending on the breeder's feeling that the puppy is not prepared for a new home and adventure. Puppies lovingly nurtured and initially socialized by their breeders usually thrive when they join their new families and throughout their lives. Puppies from puppy mills are usually removed from their dams prematurely and often never enjoy critical early socialization. Consequently, they are far more likely to become neurotic as they mature.

When owners bring their puppy home, they begin making adjustments that imprint their lifestyle and family routines on each other. The joys and struggles of this initial period provide the emotional glue that seals a lifelong love affair for most. This bonding opportunity optimally occurs from about 8 to 11 weeks of age, as most Bull Terrier puppies are dealing with confidence and attachment issues that are critical at approximately that age. Owners tend to cherish early memories of their cute, chubby, confident baby. If the window of time shifts, some owners don't seem to develop that crucial initial attachment to the puppy.

Paperwork

When buying a puppy, a new owner should pay for the puppy only when proper documentation has been produced. The breeder will have already registered the litter and will fill out the AKC's Dog Registration Application with you. Read it carefully and ask the breeder to help you complete it. If you have an agreement to co-own the puppy, the breeder will have already done most of this. It's critical that buy-

Carefully read, prepare, and sign all contracts and AKC registration forms.

ers work with breeders they trust and that they examine paperwork carefully. When the buyer has had a chance to carefully review the individual Dog Registration Application and AKC pedigree, breeder contracts, and testing documentation, then it is time to sign agreements and pay. The AKC is exacting in their requirements for accurately completed registrations. Be certain that the AKC form and any breeder agreements are carefully and fully completed. Both breeder and buyer should have copies of the form as submitted to the AKC, whether mailed, faxed, or completed online. Then it's time to take the puppy home to a new and wonderful adventure with his new family.

Understanding the AKC Standard and Why You Care

The importance of family bonding and love can never be underestimated. A puppy is handed from a good breeder to an owner charged with the care and guidance of that puppy's life!

Whether seeking a show or a pet Bull Terrier, buyers and owners should recognize that the AKC standard serves as an important guide to the physique and basic persona of the breed. Many wrongly believe that AKC standards are important to only those who show. The standard outlines what the dog should look like and gives important guidance in understanding what amounts to quality and soundness in the breed. Every Bull Terrier owner and potential owner should care enough to be knowledgeable of the standard and what it means. When looking at puppies, smart potential buyers will go armed with a copy of the standard, which can be found at *http://www.akc.org/breeds/bull_terrier/index.cfm*, and ask the breeder to discuss it with them, particularly in terms of how the puppy is liable to measure up. Those most interested in pet puppies should ask why a particular Bully is considered pet quality.

Introduction and Body Description

The first paragraph is an important introduction that speaks to the essence of the breed. The standard then provides a rather complete description of the head, which is an important component of the breed, and progresses to discuss the body build and movement. The standard describes healthy adult physique and temperament. Allowance must be made for puppies, but the standard serves as a basic point of reference for determining quality or lack thereof. For example, buyers should understand that blue eyes are an undesirable disqualification, but some puppies have a bluish cast in their eyes that disappears at an early age.

From puppies to adults, Bull Terriers love to have fun!

Generally, there is a reason that points outlined in the standard were developed. Taken as a whole, they create a portrait of the correct, quality Bull Terrier. Understanding the standard means that a buyer has a basis for analyzing the parents, deciding which puppy to select, and whether any of the puppies offered should be considered.

How to Show

The standard also offers clues as to how to best show a Bull Terrier, highlighting positives and deemphasizing points that are perhaps less than truly desirable as outlined in the standard. While there is no perfect Bull Terrier, the standard's guidance can help the prospective owner analyze how closely a puppy or dog might

measure up in terms of being a good-looking representative of the breed.

Finding Love with a Mature Companion

Adopting an Adult

Many people are busy and don't really have time or energy to train and keep up with a puppy. Sometimes puppies are hard to find, as good breeders often have waiting lists. Some people are not able or willing to pay the going rate for a puppy. An attractive option that should be explored is to look into adopting an adult Bull Terrier.

Some breeders will occasionally have an adult Bull Terrier available. The dog may be a retired show dog or one who was returned after the death of a co-owner, or because of a friend's inability to care for the dog. Bull Terriers are not good pack animals and do not do well in kennels. They earnestly need human companionship and to be part of a family. Good breeders usually try to limit the number of Bull Terriers they keep, so that each gets quality time and attention; consequently, Bull Terriers are rarely kept in real kennels.

Rescue: The Bull Terrier Club of America and each regional club have rescue organizations, working to save and rehome purebred Bull Terriers. While breed rescue does have some younger dogs, most are adults of varying ages. Bull Terrier clubs and rescue organizations are almost always looking for good permanent and foster homes for these wonderful dogs. These rescues need homes for a variety of reasons. Some are well trained and healthy. Some need special care and training. Most are sensitive and need reassurance and consistency, much like adopted human children do.

Clubs temperament-test each Bull Terrier being sponsored, update vaccines, and verify any health issues. They will also attempt to match families to Bull Terriers that will be best suited to the family's lifestyle and expectations. Everything known about the dog and her background will be carefully discussed with potential adoptive families. Families will be required to complete applications. Generally, a house check will be conducted by a club member. An adoption fee helps the club cover some of the expense of testing and caring for the dog. Some Bull Terriers come from atrocious situations and need experienced, sensitive care. Others were well cared for and adapt to new surroundings and family easily. Most Bull Terriers are surprisingly resilient. They are virtually never one-person dogs and tend to adjust to new lives and new rules with time and persistence. Most find that giving hope to and living with a rescued Bull Terrier is one of the most tremendously rewarding experiences of a lifetime.

Those willing to provide loving care, careful guidance, and a fun, interesting, comfortable lifestyle should apply. The national rescue hot line is *1-800-BTBT-911*. Additional information can be obtained at *http://btca.com/rescue/index.html*

Those who want to make a difference in the world should consider adopting or fostering one of these wonderful Bull Terriers. The love and happiness you give these dogs will be returned a hundredfold.

Sometimes the most precious of our friends are mature and senior Bull Terriers. They are like treasures at the end of a rainbow.

TRAINING BASICS OR BASIC TRAINING

When owners understand the need for and begin training and socialization, Bull Terriers are among the most rewarding, amusing breeds to work with and love. The basic premise for successful training of Bull Terriers is to make the entire experience fun!

Being Successful

Clear direction and positive reinforcement, patience, and a ready smile will effect real progress, if not wonders. A trainer who is inconsistent or who isn't carefully listening to himself and observing the youngster's reaction will find that most Bull Terriers will respond by wanting to play or by wanting to go take a nap.

For success, a trainer needs to have the puppy's attention. If a puppy is tired or keyed up and in need of a walk, attention is not what a trainer will get. Also fundamental to success is the realization that teaching and learning are an every-moment occurrence. Good breeders begin training with very young puppies and hand off puppies to new families with guidance and ideas for continuing education.

Most quality Bull Terriers are good mothers and good puppy managers!

Rewards

To most Bull Terriers, the really precious rewards are praise, laughter, play afterward, and delicious treats. Experienced trainers know that food treats should be varied and offered somewhat sparingly. Vocal praise must be given quickly and sensitively in response to achieving the behavior that is desired. Taking time to play afterward seals a good experience in a youngster's mind. Because play is so important to young Bullies, they often work harder to please, so they can finish and chase a tennis ball.

It All Starts with Mom

Training begins in the whelping box and is managed by the puppies' mother and by the breeder. Essentially, neonate puppies learn pack behavior and who to trust and follow. Breeders who carefully handle their puppies in introduc-

Routines and praise are critical components of puppy training.

ing them to their place in this world are very important in setting puppy paws in the right direction. Most breeders also understand how readiness to learn affects each puppy individually and will discuss that and the puppy's history, when she goes to her new home.

As puppies grow, the ultraimportant, fundamental rules that owners must recognize involve the pack nature of all dogs. Essentially what this means is that a Bull Terrier puppy needs clearly to know who is in charge and that it is not her. Owners must establish that all humans in the family have pack priority over all canines. Bull Terriers, who see that their leader or leaders are confidently providing for them, are happy dogs and family members. When there are multiple

dogs in the household, owners must learn to understand and recognize the pack order within the canine members of the family. The human leader is responsible for respecting their pack order while ensuring honorable, safe, fair treatment for each member of the pack.

House-training

Puppies have a natural tendency toward cleanliness; they will move away from their sleeping area to urinate or defecate. As babies they have minimal control, in part because their bladders and bowels are small. Once they are weaned, good breeders gradually begin to help them learn a variety of useful behaviors including elimination control. Patience and a positive approach are absolutely required.

✔ Puppies should have an established sleeping area, which is kept clean, warm, and dry.

✔ A separate eating area should be nearby.

✔ Newspaper should surround the bedding and dining areas, principally covering play and exploring areas.

✔ Papers should be changed daily, keeping the area around the dining and sleeping areas clean and especially sanitary—puppies learn to go further and further from their personal nest for elimination.

✔ Once puppies reach about five weeks, papers can be moved back slowly (day by day) to the corner of the puppy area.

✔ After puppies eat, they should be taken outside immediately. Praise for eliminating outdoors should be lavish!

✔ Puppies need appropriate exercise, allowing them to use their growing body and eliminate appropriately.

Note: Punishment has NO part in housetraining. Training must be consistent, positive, and progressive.

Schedules

Keeping a regular schedule is enormously helpful. When first getting up in the morning, the owners should tiptoe down to where the puppy is sleeping and as she wakes up, quickly take her outside for the first bathroom break. Owners can't stop for coffee. A puppy needs to

Short, regular daily training, plus conformation and/or obedience classes with local kennel and dog training clubs, are critical to establishing good habits and behavior.

get out immediately. Using the same approximate area each day helps establish in the puppy mind that this is an approved place for her use.

Accidents

Puppies will have accidents. Old methods such as shoving their nose in the urine or swatting them, is not very effective and is generally confusing to the puppy. An owner observing a puppy urinating, should yell loudly, swoop up the puppy and take her outside. The owner must stay outside with the puppy until she urinates again. The owner then offers enthusiastic praise and pats and hugs because the puppy has done the right thing in an acceptable place—only then do puppy and owner return to the house.

To remove temptation and confusion, the soiled area inside should be carefully cleaned and sprayed with an odor-removing agent. The puppy is learning the relationship between her feeling of needing to void, location importance, and how to please her pack leaders.

Good training starts early and is consistent.

Command words: Owners can also begin to teach a term or a short command that will be associated with a bathroom break, such as *"Do your duty."* Obviously this can be handy when traveling, in cold or wet weather, but the terms must be selected carefully, so the dog is not confused later by accidental use of the term or command in daily life.

Using a positive approach, lavish verbal praise/reinforcement, attention to timing, and patience will surprise owners with how effectively and quickly puppies are house-trained. Normally, Bull Terriers are not impressed by, nor do they learn from, screaming or punishment.

A calm owner who manages the tone of his voice and is sensitive to the puppy and her psyche will be able to communicate to the puppy what behavior is appropriate and what is not.

Training Starts Early

Bully puppies experience periods of readiness, just as human children do. The perceptive owner/trainer will sense when puppies are ready to begin most training by the interest they show in toys, treats, and praise. To effectively learn, a puppy needs to feel secure and confident and consequently ready to venture and learn. Training is best accomplished when a puppy has been exercised, given a bathroom break, and before meals.

Fun Is Effective!

Training is *not* a discussion with the puppy. Good trainers are leaders who use single words to tell the dog what they expect or what is right or wrong. Start with short exercises that seem like play.

✔ Throw a ball and as soon as the Bull Terrier picks up the ball, yell and scream with enthusiasm.

✔ When she comes back, ball in mouth, to see what all the hollering is about, praise and hug her for giving you the ball. Repeat a few times.

✔ This game of "fetch" can lead to a rather easy way to begin teaching *"Come,"* by yelling *"Come"* as she reaches the ball.

✔ Praise and occasional treats are positive reinforcement. Praise should be sensitively timed and lavishly given. Food treats should be used more sparingly.

Training should be conducted in an area where the puppy can have some relative freedom, but within safe, confined limits, such as a fenced yard. Never chase a puppy that doesn't respond to *"Come."* Instead, turn and run the opposite way. Normally a Bully puppy wants to know what you are doing and she'll run after you. Since the vision of youngsters is limited, don't get too far ahead. When she catches up with you, hug and praise her.

Commands

"No"

A critical first command to teach is *"No."* Many breeders accomplish this, at least initially, with a loud "Awk" sound that puppies accept as a warning sound. Follow it by a simple *"No."*

Another technique that is very positive is to teach the puppy a word that means something wonderful is going to happen, so she'll stop and pay attention to you. We use *"What's this?"* as the first of a three-part series of commands for getting attention around home and ultimately in the show ring. Whether a puppy is thinking of snacking on a poisonous plant or approaching one of those cute black and white kitties (otherwise known as skunks) in the yard, a loud *"What's this?"* will attract her attention.

"Sit"

"Sit" is one of the easiest commands to teach. Start by getting the puppy's attention with a treat held above her head. Move the treat slowly over her head toward her back,

"Sit" is an easy command to teach a Bull Terrier, though they often sit somewhat sideways. Teaching them to stand for examination is important for showing and non-showing Bull Terriers.

saying *"Sit."* Trying to keep the treat in sight, the puppy will sit. The instant the puppy sits, and only when she is sitting, the treat is given.

After being taught to sit, a puppy should learn to *stand on command*. This is important not only for showing, but for owner and veterinary examination. The best way to teach this skill is usually something of a reversal of teaching *"Sit."* A sitting puppy is shown a treat that is slowly drawn forward about nose height as the handler says *"Stand."* When the puppy is standing, praise and give her the treat.

Soft mouth: Carefully manage giving of treats so puppies are rewarded for being soft-mouthed. Training a puppy in calm circumstances and putting the treat at nose level, without pulling it away, tends to help keep a puppy from jumping and grabbing. Most puppies are naturally soft-mouthed, but some are not and early correction of this trait is important.

Laughter

Do not laugh at behavior that is charming in a 10-pound (4.5 kg) puppy that wouldn't be cute in a 50- or 60-pound (23–27 kg) adult.

Palming the treat so that fingertips are not exposed can help. Quick, strong words of caution should be given if the puppy seems to be snatching a treat instead of taking it nicely. Praise is critical when the puppy is gentle.

Laughter: Bull Terriers learn from laughter. These natural clowns seem to thrive on giggles and take obvious delight in getting into the strangest situations. Once a Bull Terrier learns behavior that makes her friends snicker even the slightest, she will attempt to repeat it as often as she can. The louder the chortling, the

surer the puppy is that she's done the right thing. If a Bully thinks she's entertained you by climbing on the counter and falling asleep in the sink, you will repeatedly find her snoozing in the basin.

Formal Training

In puppies, 7 to 10 weeks is an important bonding time. The 10- to 18-week period is a critical socialization and early learning time for most puppies. One of the world's foremost canine psychologists, Ian Dunbar, began a program of puppy socialization through his Sirius Training classes. This brilliant program in various forms has spread throughout the United States and is now offered in most areas, principally for puppies from 12 to 18 weeks old. Some excellent shelters such as California's Marin County Humane Society offer progressive socialization and family dog and obedience programs. Puppies and owners who participate in these programs are virtually never disappointed, as they are wonderful venues of discovery and communication. These classes are also a great way to meet other caring dog folks and are often an astonishing learning opportunity for owners as well as puppies.

Local Classes

After puppy socialization, owners should consider participating in local obedience and conformation classes. These offer not only excellent confidence, skills, and team building, they also continue to help with socialization. It is a good

Passing a treat over the puppy's head toward the rear usually results in a natural sit. The instant the puppy sits down, immediate praise is important.

opportunity to meet other breeds and their people. Most will be truly impressed with the wonderful personalities of Bull Terriers. One issue that constantly seems to be a source of comment is that most Bull Terriers do not easily do a correct obedience *"Sit."* Their physique seems to dictate that they are more comfortable in a side *"Sit."* When necessary for obedience competition, this can be corrected with positive persistence. To find obedience, agility, or conformation training, owners should contact their local kennel or dog training club for training classes. Generally, these classes are inexpensive and truly worthwhile.

Toys

Bullies of all ages tend to like to investigate their world, and many enjoy chewing. Bully puppies should be given nylabones and kongs appropriate for their size and teeth. They need to be large enough to ensure they won't be swallowed or get lodged in between the rear upper and lower molars. Most other chew toys, such as gummabones and leather chews, are not appropriate for Bull Terriers as they can too easily choke when pieces come off. All toys should be inspected daily to be sure that they remain in safe condition. Tug toys are not recommended. Toys that involve pulling can dislocate jaws and tend to unconsciously teach bad habits.

Toys must be sturdy and be inspected regularly to ensure a Bull Terrier is not liable to break or chew off and swallow any parts!

Chewing: Some Bullies are wonderful about playing nicely with their toys, others seem extremely destructive. Cloth toys are sometimes confusing to puppies as they sometimes think that couches and pillows and bedding are also chew toys. Spraying Bitter Apple on bedding or other tempting items can help discourage chewing. Bullies seem especially fond of plastic. Metal feeding dishes are recommended. Other plastic

should not be left lying about. Children's toys often have the smell of food on them that makes them even more attractive to Bullies. Children's playthings, valuables, and any tempting hazard should be placed out of a dog's reach.

Crates

Sometimes called airline kennels, these large plastic crates are great dens for Bull Terriers; they are wonderful sleeping and traveling quarters. Crates should be outfitted with clean blankets or other soft, appropriate bedding and a safe chew toy. Crates are for overnight accommodation, time-outs, and naps. Bullies should normally not be confined to them for more than eight hours overnight or a few hours during the day.

A crate is a comfortable den, whether at home or traveling!

Bedding: Bored Bullies may chew on bedding so blanket edgings should be removed. Most will not chew felted bedding and fleece materials. A Bully that tends to chew or tear up bedding often respects fleece bedding. In extreme cases, carpeting can often be securely tacked to the underside of a board that is then tightly lodged in the crate but don't use carpet that has running, continuous fibers as these can be hazardous if the dog does get even one strand loose.

Note: Many motel managers who will not otherwise accept dogs, will if owners show that a dog is sleeping in the crate, instead of on motel bedding.

Breakfast in Bed

Puppies, depending on their age, must be fed several times a day. Our adults are fed twice daily. After their morning walk, vitamins, and a bit of milk, they enjoy breakfast in their crates. The late afternoon meal is usually given in the kitchen or

A bully's crate is his den and portable, private bedroom.

in a run, but if we are traveling, those meals are also eaten in the crate. Getting the Bullies used to eating in their crates helps make them feel comfortable when traveling. If on a long drive, we can stop and feed the dogs in their crates. They are happy and we can keep driving.

Safety in Car or Air Travel

Puppies should take their first car trip in a crate when they are about six weeks old. The first drive should be short, perhaps about 10 minutes long. In a day or two, the next trip should be about 20 minutes. When the puppies are put in the crate and later when taken out, they should hear lots of praise and happy conversation. En route, puppies should enjoy music and singing. Choose your favorite radio station and let them hear classical, Western, or any pleasant music that doesn't have a heavy ominous beat. Often, the puppies will fall asleep if the driver is careful and the puppies are not tossed around. Most Bullies quickly come to love traveling. Come home and leave the tail gate open to unload groceries, and our Bullies will rush out to climb in, asking "Where are we going?"

Windows: Do not permit a Bull Terrier to hang her head out of an open window during travel. In addition to the potentially lethal temptation to jump out of the window, there is risk to eyes, nose, and ears. Windows should be closed or cracked open only slightly.

Bullies should be fastened in by a canine seat belt or travel within a crate with enough room to stand up and stretch out. Even on short trips, Bullies should be secured. A leash, water, plastic bags, bowl, and a blanket should be routinely carried in the car. Hot weather is of course the most hazardous—never leave a dog unattended in a car!

Crate Label Sample

Below is a sample of the sheet that should be printed out and securely attached to the top and back of the crate.

My Name is Pepper
I am an English Bull Terrier
I am traveling with Carolyn Alexander
to MONTEREY CA (MRY)

Tel: (831) 555-1212 home
(831) 121-5555 cell

100 Bully Street
Spreckels, CA 93962

It's my first flight!
Please take good care of me.
My Mom and Dad love me!

A comfortably large crate with contact and destination information secured to the top and back will help ensure the safe arrival of your Bull Terrier.

Airlines

Most heavy-duty plastic crates are approved for airline travel. Owners will want to double check to see that all fasteners / bolts are secure. Some add a bungee cord or tie as a double closure securing the door. Careful owners also prepare several papers that give the destination

When traveling by car, a comfortable crate or a special canine seatbelt harness is the safe way to protect your Bull Terrier.

address, the dog's name, who the dog is traveling with, cell phone numbers, and any other appropriate contact information. The owner carries the papers with return information, which replaces the outbound sheet, when departing for home or the next destination. It is also a good idea to paint the owner's name or kennel name in letters 4–6 inches (10–15 cm) high on the sides and back of the crate.

Health certificates: Within a few days of leaving on her trip, the traveling Bully needs to visit the veterinarian for a health certificate. If traveling internationally, owners will need to verify admission requirements at the overseas point of entry. Some overseas travel requires months of procedures and some testing, so advance planning is in order. Taking shot records and a first aid kit on any trip is always wise.

Requirements: When reservations are made, each airline will explain their requirements for check-in times, veterinary certificates, prior watering, and feeding. If the information is not offered, ask for details. Generally, airlines require that two bowls are attached to the inside of the crate door. Since Bull Terriers frequently will chew on and ingest plastic, stainless steel bowls that can be secured to the door should be purchased and attached in advance. *Be sure the crate has soft, safe, absorbent bedding.*

Sedation: Normally, Bullies traveling on airlines should *not* be sedated. If the dog is being

Bull Terriers love to travel, whether by car, RV, boat, or plane. They are amazingly adaptable and enthusiastic travelers.

shipped without a human traveling companion, she'll need to be checked in at the airline's baggage service center, which is normally located in a commercial runway adjacent area, rather than in the passenger terminal. Bull Terriers traveling with companions are checked in at passenger terminal airline counters.

Personnel assistence: Ask agents for their permission to walk the dog before final call for check-in or loading. Most airline personnel are caring and helpful and will try to allow time for a last walk before boarding. If a plane change is missed and a traveling dog will have extended crate time, owners should ask that the dog be brought out, so she can be walked and watered or fed. Unfortunately, security restrictions make owner access to dogs in secure areas almost impossible, so travelers must work with airline and security personnel.

If a plane change is involved, the human companion should ensure before boarding the next flight that his dog has been loaded, either by observing the loading from a window or asking the airline agent at the gate to verify that his dog has been loaded, or both. Asking the agent to certify that a crate with the name painted in large letters on the side has been loaded can help ensure that the right dog and crate have been loaded.

Children and Bull Terriers

Throughout their evolution, Bull Terriers have been known to be the dearest companions of children, perhaps because they are so childlike themselves. Families today tend to regard their Bull Terrier as one of the kids. Much like Peter Pan, a Bull Terrier never really grows up and never needs tuition for Harvard.

When traveling by plane, try to get in a last walk before final check-in or boarding.

Children and Bullies

While no child should be left alone with any dog, it is interesting to read Mitford Brice's opinion of children and Bull Terriers in 1934. "Just as the Bull Terrier is slow to anger, so he is of all terriers the one least inclined to snap, and it is probably this lack of nerves that makes him so eminently reliable with children. It is just because the Bull Terrier has the blood of a thousand fighting ancestors in his veins that he can safely be left alone with a baby and will suffer himself to be killed rather than betray his trust. A loveable gentleman is this White Cavalier, and I know no breed of dog to whom the word 'treacherous' is less applicable."

Bull Terriers develop social skills and independence at a good breeder's home. Normally they are not ready to leave the breeder until about eight weeks.

Supervision

Bull Terriers seem wonderful, natural playmates for children, but whatever the breed, children and dogs should always be supervised, sometimes to protect the dog and sometimes to protect all parties from overenthusiastic play or jealousy over a toy. Monitoring helps ensure that neither dog nor children learn bad behavior or react inappropriately. Children should be taught how to pick up and handle a puppy, and how to meet and play safely with a dog or any other pet.

As a best friend, confidante, and play pal, a Bull Terrier may decide to defend a youngster when the child doesn't need protection, as in exuberant play. Parents need to recognize, nurture, and guide the closeness that can develop between children and Bull Terriers. Bull Terriers tend to serve children as unexpectedly excellent role models and engaging companions. They offer consolation and respect. They are wonderfully sweet listeners, but usually they are not terribly good at sympathizing for very long,

The natural bond between young children and Bull Terriers is based on their mutual love of good play followed by a comfy nap.

because their outlook is so positive. Instead of letting a youngster wallow in remorse or worry, a Bull Terrier will attentively cuddle and then smile and say something like "*Wanna play?*" It's hard to mope around a Bull Terrier.

Planning for a New Bully

A Bull Terrier should be added to the family only after the family as a whole and each member individually accepts the responsibility for the care and training needed by this new family member. Children should be involved in the decision of a puppy purchase or rescue adoption through study of the breed, family discussion of needed care and routines, visits to breeders and dog shows, and Internet research. Children need to understand that the search is not *just* for a cute puppy, but for a living, loving companion, who will need their time and training, care and protection.

In meeting breeders at dog shows and at their homes, parents should note that good breeders want to meet everyone in the family and are willing to discuss puppies with the children as well as the parents. Breeders can be very helpful in preparing families for a new puppy by giving them lists of needed items, going over routines and initially explaining canine psychology. When a new puppy comes into the family, parents must be prepared to ensure that each child in the family feels involved in and participates in care of the puppy. A child who feels jealous or left out may suffer unnecessarily and react inappropriately.

Children's Books

Reading to and with young children is part of the truest joy of family sharing. Some of the finest books for children include Bull Terriers. Don't miss Lisa Kopper's *Daisy* books or Lindgren and Eriksson's *Rosa* stories, Dale's *Nipper*, Babette Cole's *True Love*, Day and Eden's *Darby*, and Silin-Palmer and Coxe's lavishly illustrated *Bunny and the Beast*. Adults love them too! Those who want their children to discover some of the old collectible stories should try to find Rosalie Mendel's delightful *Robbie* books.

Collars

• Around the house and yard, Bullies should wear a comfortable cloth collar that allows for control if you need to grab her.

• On a walk, in public areas, a strong, medium chain link collar is most serviceable.

• Lighted collars and reflective leashes are recommended for those who walk in the early and late dark hours.

• Prong collars are generally not recommended and should be used only when recommended by a professional trainer and then very sparingly.

• Use of prong collars on AKC show grounds is illegal.

• Remote shock collars should be used only with great caution and only with an adult in attendance. Shock collars that shock in response to barking are dangerous and should *never* be used.

• Citronella collars are generally safe, but don't seem terribly effective with all Bull Terriers.

• Studded, spiked collars are outdated, dramatic, and tend to evoke a fear response in observers. Bull Terriers are friendly, sweet-natured dogs and heavy-duty spiked collars are not recommended as they detract from the image of dog and owner.

• Buckled collars tend to be safe, but the adjustable quick-release, breakaway collars are more popular. They are also called quick-klip collars.

• Rolled collars tend to be more comfortable for the dog than flat ones. Buy good-quality collars that are safe, comfortable, fit well, and will last.

Remember: Puppies outgrow collars. Owners must check collars weekly to ensure that they are comfortable and safe. Some collars can be ordered with the owner's telephone number woven into the fabric. Obviously, these can help ensure the early return of a lost Bull Terrier.

Leashes

Before buying a leash, see how it feels in your hands. Many flat nylon leashes are uncomfortable and will burn hands if the dog suddenly lurches forward. Leather or medium-heavy, round nylon leashes tend to be safe and comfortable; 4- to 6-foot (1.2–1.8-m) leashes are most appropriate for everyday walking. The swivel snap quick-release hook closure tends to be more easily managed than the less popular and heavier spring snap.

Extending, roll-up leashes are useful in wide open areas, but they must be used sensibly by adults, not children. When a flexi leash is

A comfortable, short leash attached to a good quality metal choke chain is usually the best equipment for walks.

employed, the owner must be certain the leash is strong enough, correctly attached, and that the dog stays in your full control. They should not be used in busy areas with heavy traffic.

Show leashes: Show leashes are called leads and usually match the color of the dog—white leads for white Bull Terriers, black for black brindle, and brown-red leads for golden brindles and red Bull Terriers; 30- to 36-inch (76–91-cm) leads of medium-sized nylon cord are usually best for Bull Terriers. British-style slip leads, which are also called Martingales, are attractive, but should be used only on well-trained Bull Terriers being shown by experienced handlers

Exercise is an important component of a Bull Terrier's mental and physical well-being!

Muzzles

Gentle Leader and Halti collars are much like horse halters, but unfortunately, many observers think they are muzzles and a sign of a problem dog. A muzzle really can be handy to have in emergencies, as when an injured, agitated dog might need to be muzzled for safe transport to a veterinary clinic. Most muzzles do not fit the Bull Terrier's football head and can be horrifically uncomfortable, dangerous to the dog, and almost impossible to put on. Leather muzzles of correct size and some flexibility should be considered instead of wire basket models. Nylon Mikki muzzles are soft, inexpensive, and work relatively well. Still, muzzles are rarely used and can inhibit a Bull Terrier's ability to breathe. They should be used only when absolutely needed and for extremely limited amounts of time.

Fences

While not notorious diggers, Bull Terriers are ingenious escape artists. Fences and foundations around barriers should be strong and reinforced. Owners should regularly inspect fences and gates for safety and security.

Fenceless, electronic fences are limited in effectiveness with Bull Terriers that may ignore them, and totally ineffective for visiting and perhaps unwanted dogs who may come in the yard with less than honorable intentions. Owners are encouraged to consider dog runs of approximately 6 x 15 feet (1.8–4.6 m) as a safe enclosure for a dog for brief, temporary confinement as needed. The runs should be covered and located behind secure fences. The run should include a safe, dry, clean doghouse and freshly filled water bowl. Bull Terriers should be indoors in darkness and sleep inside at night.

HEALTHY, WEALTHY, AND WISE

Good health is, of course, true wealth. Wise management of health care, diet, and your Bull Terrier's lifestyle will pay enormous dividends in your dog's overall well-being and in reducing veterinary appointments and the inherent financial burden of those visits.

Basic Common Sense

Bull Terriers are truly party animals. They don't have much time for worrying about anything. Bully lives are oriented to having a good time, which means their mental health is usually in great shape. That attitude of course helps their owner's mental health too. A Bull Terrier owner's challenge is not difficult, but it is to do simple planning of diet, exercise, basic sanitation, and training that works. Bull Terriers do not require special diets or unusual exercise, so basic common sense is mostly what is required to be a successful Bully owner.

Bull Terriers love games with balls, toys, and other outdoor activities.

Feeding

Labels Can Be Your Friends

Many recent improvements in the dog food industry have resulted in safer, healthier processed foods being generally available. While many grocery stores now carry good-quality brands of dog food, feed or pet stores tend to be your best source of quality dog foods at reasonable prices. Often these stores have managers who can discuss the different brands with you and help you decide on a food to try for your Bully. Whether someone is there to talk with you or not, your best key to what you buy is your ability to read the label.

Bull Terrier adults need food that is in a normal to low protein range. They are not sporting

──── T I P ────

Pressure Cookers

Experienced chefs who cook regularly for their dogs sometimes use pressure cookers, which reduce some bones to an edible mass. Because of the extreme danger with this kind of cooker, unless directions are followed precisely it is not recommended for anyone except those who have experience and expertise in using them.

dogs that are running fields or herding dogs that are working cattle daily and need the higher-protein foods. Be wary of foods that include by-products, which can mean chicken feathers or worse. The rules for reading labels for your human family apply to reading the labels for dog food and that includes checking the expiration date.

Note: A good breeder will recommend both a high-quality puppy food and adult kibble for later use. Canned food may be used occasionally to moisten dry food, but sole use of canned food is not only expensive, it requires daily teeth brushing and doesn't allow dogs some of the chewing satisfaction they seem to enjoy.

Home Cooking

BARF: Those who like to know what is going in their dog's tummy should seriously consider doing a little home cooking for them. It can be conversion to a raw diet program, commonly known as Bones and Raw Food or *BARF*. Transition to a BARF diet should be made gradually and only after giving considerable thought to and study of managing a balanced diet for your Bully.

Stew: Another good option is to prepare a simple meal of good-quality kibble mixed with a little homemade stew. The kibble serves as the basis for the diet, but is complemented by a nutritious, interesting topping/mix. This is not to recommend the family's leftovers, though occasional adding of leftovers to a dog's meal is fine. Care must be taken to ensure that any given leftovers are suitable and safe. All food, whether homemade or purchased at a quality feed store, must be fresh, safe, clean, and nutritious.

Stew can be made once a month in a large pot in a manner of old-fashioned cooking that is easy and rather fun.

Good food, good fun, rest, exercise, and lots of love are the components of a healthy Bull Terrier lifestyle.

Fit not fat. A Bull Terrier should be substantial and in good condition, but not fat.

✔ Just put in a pound or two of meat from the grocery store; ground or fatty meats are generally not recommended.

✔ Chicken or turkey skin and excess fat must be removed prior to cooking.

✔ All bones must be removed after cooking and cooling.

✔ In addition to the meat, add several cups of rice and some clean and well-washed fresh veggies. Broccoli and carrot are great ingredients. Chopped-up potato, turnip, and most other vegetables are great additions too.

✔ Only a very small amount of spinach or garlic should be used and onion should not be used.

✔ Garlic is believed to have a natural anti-flea, anti-worm effect, but because it is in the onion family, too much could have a negative effect.

✔ Onions should be avoided, as they have been found to affect blood cell structure.

✔ Once the stew is prepared and bones removed, along with excessive fat that floats to the top, it can be packed into plastic containers and frozen.

✔ Packages can be thawed as needed to top and mix with dry quality kibble. Mixing a few tablespoons of the stew into the kibble adds a little extra interest for your Bully.

✔ Don't just put the stew on the top as the smart Bull Terrier will lick it off. Put the stew on the bottom, adding the kibble on top and stir. Some clever Bull Terriers have an innate way of knowing they should turn the bowl over to get to the good stuff. Take a few seconds and mix the stew into the dinner offering.

Bull Terriers will thrive on quality commercial foods and the addition of some nutritious home cooking, but a poor diet can result in skin problems and metabolic disorders.

Fatter Is Not Better

Well-bred Bull Terriers are by nature well-muscled, agile dogs. They need regular exercise to keep those muscles well toned. Puppy exercise should be limited to walks and play time,

Bullies usually love vitamins and pills administered in cream cheese or peanut butter.

such as throwing and retrieving tennis balls. Adult Bull Terriers need daily walks—opening the back door and letting them out in the yard does not count. Walking a couple of miles each day or a shorter walk and 20 minutes of tennis ball play should be adequate. Some Bull Terriers actually seem to like treadmills, but must always be under observation when using one.

Bull Terriers seen in the show rings are often somewhat heavier than many pets. Extra weight is often used as a technique to hide length of back. Fat must not be confused with muscle. An overweight, overfed, underexercised Bull Terrier is not healthy. The fat Bull Terrier *may* win in the show ring, but not in the long run. Owners should not hurry to put weight on young Bull Terriers. Early obesity is related to breakdown of pasterns and a variety of poor health habits that will be difficult to correct.

Pills and Peanut Butter

Vitamins may not be absolutely essential as long as puppies and adults are receiving an otherwise wholesome diet. Starting puppies with good habits is critical. Those who are administering medications in pill form or vitamins will do this in much the same way they handle giving treats. The simple secrets for giving pills and vitamins are to establish and follow a routine (such as doing things at the same time each day if you can); using the same words each time; and being very positive. If owners act like pills or going to the veterinarian or baths are something to be feared, the puppy will pick up that he is being teased or that something bad is about to happen. Smiling and acting normal, as normal as you can for being a Bull Terrier person, will help your Bully think that this is fun and part of life.

Giving pills with a bit of peanut butter or cream cheese doesn't hurt the process either. A pill wadded up in cheese will likely be spit out. A small coating of something a bit sticky such as peanut butter on a small dog cookie will hold the pill in place.

Two notes of caution: Bull Terriers should be trained to take pills only after being given permission (the "take it" command) and to take pills or treats with a soft mouth. Medications should be given only on the advice of a veterinarian. For example, over-the-counter worming medications may be unnecessary and dangerous.

Health Issues

Bull Terriers have long been listed as a breed with minimal health issues, but problems occasionally surface and a knowledgeable potential owner will want to be aware of these concerns.

Compulsive Behaviors

Compulsive tail chasing, or spinning, as it is commonly called, is a canine compulsive disorder, which is believed to have a hereditary basis. It is occasionally observed in various breeds including Bull Terriers. Since symptoms tend to be anxiety related, the dog will likely chase his tail only when stressed or involved in some kind of conflict. In calm surroundings, a dog affected by the problem may never actually

manifest symptoms. The problem has been noted to start with hormonal changes, after application of certain kinds of anesthesia, and in high-stress situations. Onset can come at any time, but is usually seen in the first year of age.

Some Bull Terriers are mildly affected and most not at all. If a dog seems interested in or wants to chase his tail, discourage him by offering a walk, suitable toys, and quiet time doing some enjoyable activity. If the dog will not be dissuaded from tail chasing, consultation with an animal behaviorist or your veterinarian is in order. Dr. Nicholas Dodman and Dr. Alice Moon-Fanelli at the Tufts University School of Veterinary Medicine have extensive experience studying this behavior.

Other compulsive behaviors occasionally found in many breeds including Bull Terriers, include obsessive licking of feet and legs, biting of flanks, snapping at imaginary flies, chasing of lights, and obsessive pacing. Whether these problems are the result of the dog reacting to

Kongs are safe toys that most Bull Terriers enjoy.

stressful situations or brain chemistry is not resolved. Owners who observe these problems should keep notes of when symptoms appear and are repeated. Identifying and reducing the source of conflict may help, as can positive training and activities that offer exercise and play with toys.

Sending, or worse, staking a dog out alone is cruel and will likely aggravate the problem. Dogs, especially Bull Terriers, need exercise with their friends and family. Owners who aren't athletic can teach the Bully to fetch and play ball. Some owners noting a dog's interest in chasing lights will use flashlights or lasers to exercise the dog and keep him amused. This is a very bad idea! Counter-conditioning and diet may also be factors in improving the dog's mental and

Young Bull Terriers especially need adult supervision. Their enthusiasm for jumping and bouncing about can result in injury, usually to their growing bodies.

physical heath and consequently reducing the evidence of symptoms. Drug therapies are also available. As in the case of any severe problem, talking with a professional is in order.

Rage or SOA

A relatively rare, but concerning problem is known as Rage Syndrome (Rage) or Sudden Onset Aggression (SOA). Believed to be related to seizure disorders and possibly inherited, it can suddenly be evidenced by even the sweetest-tempered dog. In Bull Terriers, probably the most frequent manifestation of the problem is seen when the dog is awakened suddenly. He will act aggressively toward anyone nearby, and minutes later, is calm and normal. He will seemingly not realize or remember what has happened. This problem can't be managed with retraining, because it is not a behavior issue, it is a short-circuiting in the brain, which the dog cannot control. Some drug therapies are successful in controlling the problem. Rage Syndrome is another area that has been extensively researched by Dr. Nicholas Dodman and Dr. Alice Moon-Fanelli at Tufts University. Their work was initiated by an important grant from the Bull Terrier Welfare Foundation, now sadly disbanded, but their work is continuing.

Any problem that relates to aggressive tendencies, personality changes, lack of coordination, and unusual behavior requires consultation with your veterinarian or a specialist. The problems may be related to bacterial or viral encephalitis, head trauma, brain tumor, or other factor. Not limited to Bull Terriers, a number of breeds and mixed breeds also may have seizures, with or without accompanying aggressive behavior. Anticonvulsants and other therapies prescribed by veterinarians can help resolve some of the problems. Many state universities where veterinarians are trained are sources of expert help.

Luxating Patellas and Cruciate Ligaments

Knees are important to every animal's ability to move well without pain. Patellar luxation means that the kneecap(s) slip to some degree. Whether the problem is severe or mild depends principally on the depth of the groove that holds the patella in place. The problem can be corrected surgically, but is expensive. Because good breeders have been checking sires and dams for patellar problems and screening those with the problems from their breeding programs, this is not nearly as widespread as it was two decades ago.

Owners of young Bull Terriers are advised to carefully manage them so that they don't jump down stairs, off couches, or from decks. In the developing youngster, particularly in the four- to nine-month stage, such jumps can stretch or tear cruciate ligaments. Surgery is required to repair torn ligaments, but extensive crating and rest can often result in a stretched cruciate healing itself. Veterinary consultation is mandatory if a puppy or dog goes lame for more than a few hours. Limping may also be the result of a torn toenail, a thorn, a foxtail in the foot, or worse. All need immediate attention and care.

Kidney Disease

Canine kidney problems include renal dysplasia, nephritis, and polycystic kidney disease (PKD). PKD was a serious problem primarily in Australia about a decade ago, but breeders, clubs, and universities combined forces to test and remove from the breeding program any

Caring breeders have color Doppler echocardiography performed by certified canine cardiologists to help ensure the health of offspring.

affected dogs. Through ultrasound of most affected animals in Australia and New Zealand, the problem has nearly been eradicated there. PKD has not been a known problem in the United States or Canada.

Renal dysplasia: In renal dysplasia, kidney cells do not develop properly, resulting in what is sometimes called Juvenile Kidney Failure.

Nephritis: Nephritis is an insidious problem, which is also fatal, showing up usually in adult dogs. Studies to identify DNA markers for the disease are underway. In the meantime, good breeders test any dogs that will be bred. A protein creatinine urine test with a resulting ratio of 0.3 or less is generally considered safe. Most

Caring breeders have the BAER performed at about five weeks and provide the results of this hearing test to buyers. Thanks to diligent breeders, hearing problems are diminishing.

caring owners will want to have their veterinarians run this relatively inexpensive test every year or two, whether the dog is to be bred or not. Many veterinarians offer in-house testing. In some cases, these are more expensive and less reliable than outside laboratory testing.

Veterinarians not intensely familiar with nephritis issues may recommend blood testing. Blood work is reliable for many things, but not for Bull Terrier kidney readings. Veterinarians and labs often believe that a 1.0 reading or below is satisfactory. For Bull Terriers any reading above 0.3 means they should not be bred

and that you should see a specialist for advice on diet and related issues

Heart Disease

At one time, Bull Terriers were not believed to have heart problems, but over the past two decades two principal problems have emerged as concerns. Mitral valve dysplasia essentially involves leaking between two of the heart's chambers, which results in a murmur. Subaortic stenosis is related to narrowing of the aorta. The severity of the problem determines length and quality of life. A relatively normal life is often possible with a managed diet and exercise program.

These conditions are believed to be genetic. Any dogs that are to be bred should be taken to a cardiac veterinary specialist for a full-color Doppler ultrasound. When offered at dog show clinics or through veterinary universities, the tests are often convenient and money saving. These tests are most accurately managed when administered by canine cardiac specialists, rather than general practitioner veterinarians. Auscultation or simply listening to the heart is not adequate.

Deafness

While deafness tends to be most prevalent in white animals of any species, it has also been found in colored Bull Terriers. All responsible breeders take puppies over five weeks of age for a BAER (Brainstem Auditory Evoked Response) test. Performed by a veterinarian, this is currently the definitive test for determining hearing in each ear. The test is painless and only in the rarest of cases requires that a Bull Terrier be sedated.

The breeder will receive paperwork noting the hearing capability of each ear. A copy of this

Protecting Your Bull Terrier

✔ Bedding is often the first target for a bored Bully youngster. Experienced Bully families often purchase inexpensive felted blankets that shred relatively easily and remove the binding edging, prior to being used in the crate.

✔ Carpeting made of running fibers is a terrible option for Bully households. Once the Bully starts eating a little, he may find himself unable to quit easily and will continue eating, until he has a wad of very tough string in his stomach and intestines.

✔ Keep Bullies out of the closet. Mothballs are poisonous.

✔ Flea products and many human medications are seriously dangerous to dogs.

✔ Clothing such as gloves, socks, and pantyhose are also high-risk items, which are too often left lying about.

✔ Keep Bullies out of the trash. Buttery corncobs, bones, and other great-smelling items can mean surgery, suffering, and possible death for your Bully.

✔ Chocolate, fat, fowl skin, moldy and spoiled food can all spell a serious bellyache and illness for a dog. Excessive amounts of some foods like raisins can also be surprisingly toxic.

certification should be passed along to the buyer. A dog may be unilaterally deaf, which means he is deaf in only one ear. Uni's make lovely pets, but owners will have to be aware of some limitations. The dog may not be able to hear as well or determine the origin/location of a sound. Totally deaf dogs, also called bilaterally deaf, are adoptable, but must be placed with the greatest of care. The new family must accept responsibility for teaching their deaf pet sign language and acting as ears for their pet. Neither unilaterally nor bilaterally deaf dogs should be used for breeding.

Lethal Acrodermatitis

Known generally as LAD, this metabolic disorder means that a puppy is unable to properly metabolize zinc. The problem also exists in cattle, humans, and other dog breeds. Commonly called "Zincers," the puppies are usually smaller than their littermates and often don't nurse well. If they survive the neonate stage, they will develop symptoms that include painfully sore feet and mouths, and diarrhea. The puppies often have dilute or faded-looking coats and some will exhibit serious temperament problems. Believed to be an inheritable double-recessive autosomal gene, this means that healthy parents both carry the gene, but do not exhibit any symptoms themselves. Supplementing the diet with zinc is ineffective. This condition is fatal. Most affected puppies are euthanized by two to three months of age. While some have kept Zincers alive for several years, it is a heart-breaking and debilitating condition, which results in the dog's inability to walk or grow normally.

Demodectic Mange

Tiny demodectic mites live on all animals, including humans. When an animal's immunity is lowered because of illness, stress, or rapid growth, the mites can overmultiply and do damage, principally in hair follicles. The result is hair loss and itching. Subsequent scratching causes lesions and infections. Juvenile demodex is not uncommon and is not considered a serious problem, but it should be diagnosed and treated by a veterinarian. Various treatments, good diet, and limiting stress should bring the problem under control. The hair loss/patchiness is often accompanied by a slight crusting of the skin and can be felt and seen usually on the cheeks and ear tips first. Some sufferers have a compromised immune system, which should be evaluated by a veterinarian.

Generalized demodex, while not common in Bull Terriers, has been seen in the breed. Characterized by rapidly spreading hair loss and irritation, the condition needs veterinary attention, probably on a regular and extended basis. It is treatable. Early diagnosis and treatment are strongly recommended. While this can be a serious problem, prescription medications are usually effective.

Skin Allergies or Atopy

This complex topic can best be addressed by using some common sense in both purchasing a puppy and managing care of your pet. Any animal can develop allergies. White dogs from generations of white dogs seem particularly sensitive to allergens and sun exposure. Careful breeders will not breed dogs with continual, repetitive, or serious skin problems.

Toxins: Dogs of all breeds are sensitive to lawn and pool chemicals, household cleaning compounds, and other toxins that are commonly used by almost everyone. Because they do not wear foot coverings (shoes) as we do and often lick their legs and feet, pets are often directly exposed to these toxins and are very vulnerable. Care must be taken to eliminate the sources of the potential allergens in a dog's environment.

Bathing: Frequent bathing of Bull Terriers is normally NOT the answer. Often, shampoos strip the natural oils from the skins and coats of the dogs, leaving them feeling itchy and uncomfortable. They'll roll in dirt or on carpet. They'll lick themselves trying to stop the itching. Too-frequent bathing can set up a cycle of skin reactions that will quickly spiral downward in terms of your Bully's health and happiness. A bath every six to eight weeks is pretty normal. Use only gentle shampoos and be certain that shampoos are thoroughly rinsed away (see HOW-TO: Groom a Bull Terrier for more information).

Fabric softeners: When washing dog bedding, use of fabric softeners in the water or in the dryer is not recommended. Some dogs have allergies believed to be affiliated with those softeners. Bedding should be carefully rinsed to ensure that all soap has been washed away.

Thyroid Problems

A Bull Terrier having unusual hair loss, obesity, or lethargy, or that shows aggressive tendencies may be suffering from hypothyroidism and is due for a visit to the veterinarian, who will likely recommend a blood panel, which will include testing for adequate thyroid hormone functioning. Thyroid supplements can be prescribed by veterinarians.

Cryptorchidism

Cryptorchidism occurs when one or both testicles do not descend into the scrotum; both are usually present, but one or both are retained within the body cavity. The concern is that the retained testicle will lead to cancer in the older dog, and should be checked by a veterinarian. One of the early Bull Terriers, Bar Sinister, widely believed to be a forerunner of the modern Bull Terrier, had a single testicle. Dogs must have two normal testicles to show in an AKC ring, except obedience and some veteran classes.

While not generally considered to be a serious health risk, if both testicles have not descended by six months of age, consultation with a veterinarian is in order. When a youngster is in for routine vaccinations would be an ideal time to ask the veterinarian for a full checkup. If necessary, removal of the testicles and consequent neutering is a relatively simple surgical procedure.

Owners can also gently touch the scrotal sac to determine the presence of both testicles. In fact, getting a puppy used to touching of feet, ears, mouth, and genital areas makes health checkups and showing much easier. Show dogs must stand quietly for examination of their teeth, eyes, and body. Follow any exam with praise and a treat.

Pyloric Stenosis

A relatively rare condition in Bull Terriers, pyloric stenosis has to do with the valve that controls food and water moving from the stomach into the intestines. While there is no known

Some Bull Terriers never seem to grow up and continue to explore with their mouths. They need careful supervision!

test for this condition, it can be controlled with medication. Owners of Bull Terriers that seem to vomit frequently should review the problem with their veterinarian. If pyloric stenosis is diagnosed, the dog should not be used for breeding, since the problem is believed to have a hereditary component.

Don't Eat That!

Inside

Bull Terriers, like very small children, often try to experience the world by mouthing it. Owners who do not take care to remove children's toys, which are especially enticing, or other objects from the Bull Terrier's grasp may find themselves with some real worries and some rather

Poison

If you suspect your Bull Terrier has consumed a poisonous substance or been in contact with a poisonous animal (lizard, frog, snake), contact your veterinarian, local veterinary emergency clinic, and/or the ASPCA Poison Center at 1-800-548-2423 or 1-888-426-4435

Note: The ASPCA charges a $55 flat fee per case for the call(s), so have your credit card ready. Alternately, calling 1-900-443-0000 will place the charge on your phone bill.

expensive veterinarian bills. While there is an obsessive-compulsive eating disorder called Pica, most Bull Terriers just like to *try* things.

The Yard

Watch what you put in and on your yard and what's in your driveway! Almost everyone knows that most brands of antifreeze are attractive to dogs because of the sweet taste and that antifreeze is lethal! However, cocoa mulch, many fertilizers, mouse poison and poisoned mice, slug and snail bait are also dangerous, not to mention some toads and snakes that might be wandering around. Keep dogs away from algae in standing water such as ponds or bird feeders. The latter can also be breeding grounds for some really undesirable bacteria. Many Bullies will eat grass occasionally and puppies especially like to chew. Some plants like oleander and azalea are lovely and very dangerous to consume or even taste a little.

Note: Bulbs and plants that may put your Bull Terrier at risk are detailed at *http://www. aspca.org/site/PageServer?pagename=pets_ toxicplants#G*

Diarrhea

Because Bull Terriers like to try things, owners may be faced with the occasional case of canine diarrhea. All smart owners keep a can of pumpkin in the pantry. It is usually a safe way to slow and end minor bouts of diarrhea. Other over-the-counter drugs such as Kaopectate can normally be safely used, but if diarrhea is prolonged, your veterinarian should be consulted.

Bullies of all ages tend to be curious and mouthy. Careful supervision helps keep them away from unwanted, dangerous substances.

It is also advisable to keep pediatric electrolyte fluid around the house. While in route to veterinary care, squirting a small amount of Pedialyte in the mouth of a dog suffering from diarrhea or sunstroke can be lifesaving.

If a Bull Terrier has just swallowed something such as a small toy or human medications, a call to the veterinarian or the poison control center is in order. If the veterinarian suggests inducing vomiting, about 10 ml of 3 percent hydrogen peroxide solution can be orally injected by a syringe (without the needle). Vomiting is not recommended in the case of ingestion of certain chemicals and caustics, so immediate contact with a veterinarian is imperative.

The Nosy Bull Terrier

Bull Terriers are notoriously curious and most have a strong "ratting" instinct. They will put their noses almost anywhere and, detecting something interesting, they will follow their noses down holes, around corners, and into yards and buildings. Most Bull Terriers have a "No Fear" approach to life. Most good-naturedly assume that other dogs, people, and places are fun, interesting, safe, friendly, and maybe a little exciting.

When in public areas, courteous dog owners walk their dogs on leash. Being nosy and friendly, Bull Terriers often approach other dogs, whether on leash or not. Unfortunately, many, especially those who own small dogs, often don't think leashes are necessary. Not infrequently a dog, who thinks he has something to prove, will launch an unprovoked attack upon a larger dog such as a Bull Terrier. Having your dog on leash will help control the situation and may be a critical legal element if the other dog's

Bull Terriers can sunburn and overheat. Have cold, damp towels, shelter, and Pedialyte handy on warm days!

owner claims it was the Bull Terrier that initiated the attack. Picking up your Bull Terrier while remaining calm is often the best tactic.

The Stoic Bull Terrier

Bull Terriers do not tend to complain about anything. Often, owners don't realize that their Bull Terrier is feeling poorly until the dog refuses to eat food or drink water, or can't get up, or faints. Owners must be sensitive to small changes in behavior. Bull Terriers are generally quite hearty, healthy dogs, whose approach to life is "Is it fun? Then let's do it." If they are happy and enjoying life, they may not let owners know they are feeling ill until the situation is serious. Weekly checks of ears, eyes, teeth, and feet, and daily observation of behavior are early clues to potential concerns.

Sun Exposure

White Bull Terriers are especially sun-sensitive and many seem to love to sunbathe. Sunscreen lotions for dogs are now readily available, but owners must be cautious about having their Bullies out in the noonday sun because of the risk of sunstroke as well as sunburn. Having damp towels in an ice chest, ready to cover the dog while standing by for the show ring or at the beach, is very smart. Having shade in the yard or on a picnic is smart for people and Bullies. Often an owner doesn't know a Bull Terrier is in trouble until the dog keels over. Small amounts of pediatric electrolyte fluids squirted in the dog's mouth and application of cold towels on his abdomen and feet, while getting him in the shade, will help until the veterinarian arrives.

A Friend You Can Count On—the Veterinarian

Finding a veterinarian who loves Bull Terriers and who is interested in discussing problems,

conditions, and options for care is an extremely important step in any health program. Usually your breeder can recommend a veterinarian or find a recommendation for you. One of the benefits of joining a regional Bull Terrier Club is that you can ask other members which clinics they like and why. Your primary factors in finding a good veterinarian are proximity and the talent and personality of the veterinarian.

Hours: Consider also the hours of operation. Many veterinarian offices now have weekend hours, which can mean fewer emergency calls and extra charges.

Fees: Ask the veterinarians about fees and charges, and whether they take credit cards.

The Clinic

Visit the clinic. It gives you an initial opportunity to see if the staff is friendly and cheerful. Look at the waiting room and get an idea of how important cleanliness might be to the staff. Young puppies should only visit the veterinarian as necessary. Wise owners will hold them or bring them in a clean box, rather than allow them to walk through waiting room areas. Bringing a clean towel from home to put on the examination table can also help minimize the risk of contact with viruses and bacteria. Once the first sets of shots have been given, an owner might ask the veterinarian about an occasional free, walk-in visit just to say hello, so that your Bull Terrier comes to the clinic just to meet the staff and get a treat. He will then begin to feel that veterinary visits can be fun and tasty, rather than be feared!

Early checkups help keep puppies healthy and help them to establish a good relationship with their veterinarian.

Teaching your Bull Terrier to stand for examination is also helpful.

Note: Ask how emergency care is handled and be certain that if your veterinarian doesn't handle after-hours emergencies, you know the way to the clinic that does. The phone numbers for your veterinarian(s) and the nearest emergency clinic should be posted by your telephone(s).

More than One Veterinarian

Some veterinarians are specialists. Often you may find that you like different veterinarians for different procedures. A local veterinarian may be wonderful for basic care and consultation, another veterinarian may be best for surgical procedures and offer low-cost X-rays and ultrasounds. Having more than one veterinarian is perfectly acceptable. Additionally, many low-cost vaccination clinics are often held in pet food stores. Sometimes they include procedures such as microchipping, fecal sample checks, and other relatively routine veterinary services. Utilizing different veterinarians and services means that owners must carefully keep all records of vaccinations and procedures, as the dog's records are not centralized at one office.

A Word About Vaccines

Your breeder and veterinarian will recommend schedules for the various vaccinations. In some states, the law sets vaccine protocol, usually in regard to rabies inoculation. If your puppy has come from a breeder whose home is scrupulously clean and well kept, you should feel comfortable taking the breeder's advice on vaccine schedules. Normally a puppy will not leave the breeder's home unless he has had one shot for canine distemper, adenovirus type 2,

Discuss your Bull Terrier's environment to help determine what vaccines are needed.

and parvovirus at approximately seven to eight weeks and a second scheduled at approximately nine to ten weeks. Those three shots are considered to be essential protection for all dogs and should be kept current.

Often packaged with them is a less critical, but sometimes useful inoculation for parainfluenza, and distemper measles. Whether these need to be or should be administered should be discussed with your veterinarian.

Some owners and veterinarians prefer to give separate shots rather than the multivalent shots, citing various rationales. However, most

TIP

Vaccines and Medications

Keep records on vaccines and medications handy. Carry the information, copies of vaccination certificates, and your veterinarian's telephone number with you on trips.

veterinarians and breeders agree that the combined shots are perfectly safe and as effective as vaccines that are individually given. The principal difference is that individual injections will

usually cost more and represent additional invasive procedures. It is a good idea to ask your veterinarian to give you proof of precisely what vaccine was administered.

Rabies vaccines: Dr. Jean Dodds, a noted research immunology veterinarian, has suggested that rabies vaccines should *not* be administered at the same time as other vaccines, which is another topic for discussion with your veterinarian. The timing of rabies vaccinations varies somewhat, but the first is usually given between four and six months of age. After one year of age, a dog can be vaccinated yearly or every third year, depending on the type of vaccine used. The multiple-year vaccine is safe and usually more cost effective. Since state law and/or local statutes often cite specific requirements for the rabies vaccine, such as who can legally administer the shots and ages of dogs required to have the shots, owners will want to verify what is mandatory. Whether compulsory or not, the rabies shot is generally considered safe and an easy, inexpensive form of protection for any dog.

Lyme vaccine: Because of controversy regarding the Lyme vaccine, owners and their veterinarians should carefully consider whether that inoculation is truly needed. Bull Terriers that live in or near wooded areas or that go hiking and camping with their families are potential candidates for the Lyme vaccine.

Leptospirosis: Leptospirosis vaccine cannot safely be administered before a puppy is 12 weeks old. Lepto problems vary by area and living condition of the pet. This controversial vaccination should be discussed with your

Bull Terriers can be trained and enjoy showing.

Discuss your Bull Terrier's lifestyle with your veterinarian. It can make a difference in the vaccines recommended.

veterinarian. The lepto vaccine is often recommended for dogs that live in barns, possibly have contact with mice, rats, and cattle, or are exposed to contaminated water.

Important! Owners who are not conversant with the most current information in vaccines should not administer them without supervision of a veterinarian and/or doing careful research. Most owners prefer to go to a veterinarian or clinic, rather than administering shots themselves, but the owner is always ultimately responsible for keeping careful records on shots given and when due next. Current thinking is that vaccines for corona, giardia, or adenovirus type 1 should not be routinely administered, if at all. It is always wise to discuss an overall

health program with an interested, up-to-date veterinarian.

Bordetella: Most kennels require proof of bordetella vaccination before they will accept an animal for boarding. Bordetella is the most common cause of tracheobronchitis, commonly called kennel cough. Because kennel cough is a bacterial-borne illness and extremely contagious, many show dogs are bordetella vaccinated. Normally, really young puppies are wisely kept near their own homes, where the risk should be minimal. Usually, veterinarians or breeders don't administer bordetella vaccines until a puppy is at least three months old, and it should normally be readministered to healthy at-risk dogs every six months. This particular

A healthy, happy Bull Terrier is a joy to behold.

vaccine may be administered through injection, which is believed to last longer. It may also be squirted into the dog's nose. The process is called *intranasal* and is believed to convey quicker immunity.

Senior Dogs

Current veterinary thinking is that many senior dogs do not require annual boosters and overvaccination of aging dogs may be counterproductive to their health. Rabies is often required by law, but other preventive boosters deserve a serious discussion with your veterinarian. New technology is now offering serum testing, which determines the immunity levels of an animal. This testing will eventually become more common and allow dogs to be vaccinated only for protection needed.

Critters

Fleas and ticks are problems in almost every part of the world. Thanks to relatively new products and methods of monthly control, these beasts are more easily controlled than in our parents' time. Owners should discuss flea control with their veterinarians and read advertising and comparison literature to decide which form of control is best for their pet. Reading pet supply catalogs is often a good way to learn about and compare products and pricing.

Worms

Curious puppies rather easily pick up internal parasites such as hook-, whip-, and roundworms by contact with contaminated materials. Tapeworms often are associated with a flea problem, but can be picked up from contact with contaminated fecal material and meat. Fresh fecal samples should be taken to your veterinarian probably every six months to verify that your pet is free from debilitating worms. Usually, good veterinarians don't charge an office visit for a fecal check. If parasites are identified, owners should absolutely follow the advice and prescription provided by their veterinarian. Over-the-counter medications should be administered only by the most experienced and knowledgeable breeders, most of whom choose veterinarian supervision.

In puppies at least three weeks of age, most breeders will administer a prophylactic dose of a safe wormer made from pyrantel paomate. While safe, directions must be followed carefully. Prophylactic essentially means that the medicine is given just in case the puppies have worms. In a litter situation, it is hard to determine which droppings are from which puppies and parasites can be so easily spread that worming of the entire litter with a safe product is usually a very good idea.

Heartworm is carried by mosquitoes and is of special concern in areas frequented by these pesky varmints. Veterinarians can advise on the heartworm risk in your area. Generally a conservative approach to putting chemicals into you or your dog is advised, but heartworm is so insidious and the curative is so risky that it is important that you seek your veterinarian's advice in this regard.

A Partnership

Recognize that although most health care professionals also want the best for your Bull Terrier, not all agree on the best vaccination protocol. Owners need to be prepared to knowledgably discuss health care issues with their breeder and veterinarian. Real health is achieved through good breeding practices, a program of healthy diet and exercise, qualified veterinary care, and a sensitive, caring owner. Some carefree playtime and rest are also important parts of the healthy lifestyle equation. Good mental health is also achieved through positive training and participation in family activities. Having a healthy, loving friend is in the long run far more valuable than great wealth, and your Bull Terrier can be one of the best of friends.

Adult Bull Terriers make wonderful companions and are often available from breeders and rescue.

Bathing Beauties

Because of their short coat, Bullies are sometimes referred to as "wash and wear dogs," as they are easier to groom than most breeds. As a rule, frequent baths are not required and are not best. Over bathing and use of harsh, perfumed shampoos can contribute to skin irritation and set up a cycle of skin problems. Veterinarians often respond to skin problems with more shampoos, prednisone, and other techniques. The additional shampooing may actually make the problem worse, and prednisone is a steroid that masks the itching problem. The best solution is to keep skin problems from starting.

Read labels. Some shampoos are not safe for puppies. Use a good-quality skin-sensitive dog shampoo. Rinse thoroughly! Conditioners are unnecessary.

Start trimming nails as early as needed. A calm, easygoing approach usually helps the Bull Terrier relax.

Put a non-slip mat on the tub floor. Be sure the water is slightly warmer than the dog's normal body temperature of 101°F (38.3°C). Keep a hand on the dog while bathing to reduce shaking.

Shampoo around the neck first to help prevent any fleas from trying to hide in the dog's ears. Then shampoo the body, and finally the head. Minimize the amount of water in the ears and eyes. Talk to your Bully; soothe his fears. Dry carefully, especially the ears. Afterward, offer a treat with lots of praise.

While bathing should be relatively infrequent, ears, eyes, mouth, and the general body should be checked weekly. Brush your Bully's coat weekly with a medium soft brush or knobby glove to reduce shedding and keep his coat shining.

Nails

Nails should be trimmed as needed. Bullies who run, walk, and play on rough, hard surfaces seem to need less nail filing than others. Diet and genetics are also likely components in how often you'll need to file nails. A Dremel-type tool with a small grinding head is easiest on everyone and not as likely as cutting tools to cause bleeding or cracking of nails.

The key is to start young, keep everything easygoing, and reward the Bully with a treat afterward.

Smile

Begin teeth brushing when the Bully is a puppy. Use only canine toothpaste and brushes as human toothpaste can sicken a Bully. Fingertip brushes are often easiest to use. Reward with lavish praise. Veterinary visits should include a dental checkup. Professional cleaning may be needed occasionally.

Grooming Table

Grooming tables allow the owner to place the Bully at eye level for basic grooming and maintenance. Patting the tabletop and putting a treat on the table about 2 inches (5 cm) from the edge will encourage an adult Bully to put his front legs up to see if he can reach the treat. When his front legs are up, lift the rear legs and reposition him on the table. Put his head in the table's noose and offer lavish praise. The noose should be snug, but not tight. Never leave a Bull Terrier unattended for even a moment on a table! Jumping off or turning it over can result in serious injury. At least one adult must be next to the table at all times!

TERRIER

Ears

Ears should be checked weekly and cleaned as needed. Bull Terriers are not prone to ear infections, but they tend to need their ears cleaned with some regularity. Gentle cleaning with tissues and swabs are preferable to many commercial chemical potions, which tend to have a drying effect on the ears. If an ear seems infected, a trip to the veterinarian's office will

When taping ears, use breathable tape.

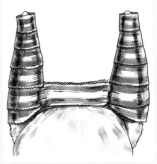

Wrap gently so that circulation is not affected.

provide the needed analysis and medications for correcting the problem.

Medications: Ear medications are most easily administered outdoors where the dog's natural shaking response won't throw ear debris around the home. Ear medications or cleaners must be at least room temperature or slightly warmer. After any shaking, the ear area should be cleaned with a soft tissue. Afterward, praise liberally and offer a treat.

Ear Taping

Puppies are born with soft, dropped ears. Often when they go home at about eight weeks, their ears are not yet erect. Good breeders will discuss the need for *natural* calcium in the diet and taping ears if they are not up by about 12 weeks.

Methods vary: Some employ small wood Popsicle sticks and moleskin attached to the inside of the ear. Others use forms cut from Styrofoam, smaller than the ear leather, attached to the interior of the external ear with waterproof glue. We have had the best luck using paper tape, which can be removed with minimal hair pulling, and a soft form for inside the ear. This form can be cut from foam rubber. Tampons can also be used so long as they are not deodorized or ultra

compact. Two people are required, one to hold and control the puppy, and one to face the puppy and do the taping.

Taping begins at the base and circles up around the ear almost to the tip. Tape must be applied with gentle firmness, but must not be tight! When both ears are taped, a piece of tape should be placed across the upper portion of the ears connecting them. This bridge helps support both ears in an upright position. When finished, the puppy should be praised and receive a treat. The puppy is likely to scratch the back of the ears. If the area becomes irritated a tiny touch of antibiotic cream will help it heal. Take care to use a very small amount as most of these ointments have some toxicity if ingested.

Replacing tapes: The puppy may remove the tapes; replace them if the ears are not up. Once he has worn the tapes for three to five days, remove them. If the ears are still not up, tape them again after two days. Repeat as often as necessary. Check the tapes every day. If any foul odor or swelling is noted, a trip to the veterinarian is in order. When puppies are teething at approximately four to six months of age, ears may go soft again and require some short-term taping.

HAVE YOU HAD YOUR PLAY TODAY?

Bull Terriers sometimes seem to be difficult, even stubborn, but owners must recognize that a principal driving force in their makeup is the desire to play and have a great time.

Probably the single most compelling reason to own a Bull Terrier is to put some fun into each and every day of your life. Busy with our hectic lives, we find that Bull Terriers tend to make us stop and put us back in touch with our inner child. They also nurture us by making us realize that we are needed, that our smiles are appreciated, and our love is returned. Bull Terriers with their silly antics keep us amused, humble, and in touch with the simple, healing nature of laughter.

Laughter

Everyone loves puppies, which is good because Bull Terriers tend to have a prolonged

Bully puppies are curious, mischievous, clownish performance artists.

puppy personality. When they grow to adulthood, they may show their maturity through size and coordination, but inside every Bully is a puppy just waiting for an opportunity to play. Most adult Bull Terriers put up with a certain amount of boredom, but despite the development of some patience, their prime directive is to have a good time and hang out with folks who like to enjoy life.

A critical training element has to do with laughter—it must not be forgotten that a Bull Terrier loves laughter. It is tantamount to sincere praise to them. It will reinforce behavior more quickly than anything, including much desired treats. Those who laugh at the antics of a 10-pound (4.5-kg) puppy may have to deal with that behavior in a 60-pound (27-kg) adult dog. Perhaps advice should be in the category of "Be careful what you wish for." Sensitive owners will want to correct bad behavior, no

Bull Terriers love playing "king of the mountain" and doing anything that seems fun!

matter how charming in a puppy, with verbal disapproval and body language. However, first they may want to grab the camera to take a photo to show friends that the puppy really did climb into the bird cage and fell asleep with the bird perched on her head. Bull Terriers really do require monitoring. They are very much like small children most of their lives and often innocently get themselves in compromising and even dangerous situations. Actually, it might be better said that they are like small children who want to grow up and be on the Comedy Channel.

Roles

Therapy dogs: Once a new Bull Terrier owner relaxes and understands that Bullies are strongly motivated by fun and laughter, they usually start to participate in enjoying their own lives more. Bull Terriers are often trained and certified as therapy dogs, visiting hospitals and senior homes. However, Bull Terriers are special masters at therapy for their owners, who love and accept their proclivity for human interaction and companionship.

This is not to say that a Bull Terrier will not comfort the grieving or attempt to please in other ways, but generally, she thinks that the best way to extend sympathy is by getting her family to enjoy the basics, like good food and good fun. Bullys seem to know that sadness can

Puppies start with off-leash training and play, and then progress to leash training, with playtime afterward as a reward.

be averted by a walk in the sunshine, a visit to the park, or a special treat.

Watchdog: Sometimes, a Bull Terrier will make a somewhat pitiful attempt at being a watchdog. This is usually accomplished as the dog has been asleep on the couch for an hour or so, opens one eye, and rouses herself to bark a couple of times so that everyone knows she's on duty, followed by an immediate return to somnolence. Those wanting a real watchdog would not find this amusing, but Bull Terrier people smile and enjoy the performance art.

Versatility: Bull Terriers are also inspirational personalities. A hearty breed physically, mentally, and emotionally, they can endure some really difficult situations and many have survived truly inhumane circumstances. Amazingly, when rescued, even the most abused tend to eventually rebound, showing their childlike trusting, inquisitive, playful natures. People are often amazed at the versatility and persistence of a Bull Terrier. Their ability to survive and retain a positive outlook is inspiring.

A Good Citizen

Canine Good Citizen (CGC) is a fundamental program that teaches and demonstrates canine good manners and responsible dog ownership. The AKC's 10-step test is generally considered the first and most basic stage for establishing a solid foundation for participation and achievement in other performance activities. CGC pays big dividends in owner-dog bonding, behavior, and self-esteem and can serve as an initial defense if a dog is accused of bad behavior.

The Agile Bull Terrier

The original function of early Bull Terriers required a certain amount of agility and purposeful body control. Whether they were ratting or lounging on the couch, Bull Terriers over the ages have found ways to enjoy life and enjoy living in their bodies. They seem to take pleasure in physical and mental challenges, as long as they are having fun. Today, Bull Terriers enjoy agility and rally.

In training for agility, the required *down stay* is possibly the most difficult for them; everything else is fun, fun, fun. It's great exercise for a Bull Terrier and owner and participation is generally encouraged by breeders and trainers. A cautionary note, however, is age-related. Young Bullies, whose bones are developing and who are growing rather rapidly, may not be well suited to some of the jumps. Experienced trainers recognize potential hazards and usually warn those

Most Bull Terriers love to play with other dogs. Play should be encouraged, but adult supervision is advised.

explain an activity that is to be performed. The activities vary by level of expertise and competition. Handlers and dogs proceed briskly, but pretty much at their own pace. Handlers can encourage their dogs through praise and are penalized for intimidating tactics. Rally is enormously popular and seems a perfect venue for Bull Terriers and their people.

Obedience

Obedience is structured, multi-level testing that challenges the individual dog and owner to learn to work with each other and meet the established criteria for certain positive behavioral tasks. While Bull Terriers enjoy athleticism and mental stimulation, obedience is not always easy for them. As thinking dogs, in mid-exercise they will begin to reflect on how charming the nearby Newfoundland looks and whether he might like to go out for a stroll, instead of the accuracy of the procedure in which she is involved. Dedicated Bull Terrier enthusiasts have worked with their charges to win well-deserved obedience titles, but it is not easy. The obedience trainer must inspire his Bull Terrier to believe that obedience is really fun and that a significant reward follows excellent performance.

Despite being known as couch potatoes, Bull Terriers need exercise and activity, too!

with large-boned youngsters to train in only areas that are less stressful to growing bodies.

Rally

Rally is one of the newest AKC events; it calls for genuine teamwork between the Bull Terrier and her handler. It is less structured and less rigorously scored than obedience or agility. Signs at each of several designated stations

The Shows

Differences in Shows, Matches, Judges

Matches are held by clubs principally to offer training opportunities for young dogs and novice owners in a realistic show environment. Matches are also wonderful social occasions to meet other dog people and enjoy sharing the day with your dog. Essentially, matches vary by whether they are given by a breed club or a kennel club. A kennel club usually offers conformation competition and obedience for all AKC breeds, complete with Group and Best in Match competition. Bull Terrier clubs offer matches that are for Bull Terriers only. Often they include picnic lunches, rescue parades, club meetings, and raffles for unique breed items, as well as a chance to meet others and train your Bully. Most offer nice breed-relevant trophies and prizes as well as ribbons. Most Bull Terrier clubs hold these matches once or twice every year.

Handling: Handling classes are offered at some matches and by all breed clubs. In showing dogs, people must first learn the words, moves, and procedures. Once the handler starts to understand what to expect and how to react, teaching Bull Terriers is actually quite easy. The idea is to relax, and have a good time, while teaching them that showing can be fun.

Most matches are not just for puppies. Usually, adult and sometimes veteran classes are offered. It's all fun and not very serious. Breeders usually come and help owners evaluate puppies and over lunch or snacks discuss upcoming shows, training, and diet. Owners are encouraged to show their youngsters and have a good time. While there is an element of competitiveness, the key is keeping things fun and relaxed. Winning is related to the quality of the dog, showmanship, and the judge's interpretation of the standard. Whether winning or not, an owner-handler can enjoy learning and working with his dog.

Judges: Judges at matches and sweepstakes are usually breeders or AKC judges, who are not yet certified to judge that breed or breeds. Matches represent a valuable learning opportu-

Fresh air, sunshine, and a little romp with friends make life fun for a Bully!

nity for them also and are part of preparation for judging the breed and awarding points.

Sweepstakes: Sweepstakes are also offered at some AKC shows. These are sponsored by the Bull Terrier Club of America (BTCA) or the regional Bull Terrier club. AKC points are not awarded, but usually nice breed trophies are. Intended as a fun, learning experience for young dogs and owners, these are enjoyable and present a great opportunity to train, learn, have fun, and win some prizes. Afterwards, clubs often have other social events such as luncheons,

Young Bull Terriers and their owners will always find enjoyment showing in Sweeps and Matches.

and that the judge may be, but probably is not, a Bull Terrier specialist. Nevertheless, the judge will be certified to judge the breeds which are scheduled. Going to any show with friends and family is always enjoyable. While food is available at the shows, taking a picnic lunch often makes the occasion more festive and relaxing, while saving money. If you win, you'll want to wait to show in Group against the other Terriers, so having lunch or snacks and some folding chairs along can make the day more relaxing and comfortable.

Show Time

✔ Whether your scheduled show time is 8 A.M. or 1 P.M., it's a good idea to arrive at least an hour early, so that you have time to park, find your ring, check in—get your arm band and let the steward know you are there—and get yourself and your dog settled. It's a good idea to bring the dog's crate and bedding; she'll be more comfortable traveling and waiting. A Bully's crate is usually a large one, so having or purchasing a cart to haul the crate is a very good idea.

✔ In addition to treats for the dog, owners will want to have a show collar and lead. Show collars for Bull Terriers are usually small link choke chains, which are strong enough to hold the dog, but are not overlarge. The collar should slip over the head of the dog easily, but when slightly tightened around the dog's neck should not show length over about 3 inches (7.6 cm) above the neck. Show leads should match the dog's coat color. In other words, black for black brindles, red/brown for red, dark brown for

cocktail or wine and cheese parties, raffles, and lots of time to talk about dogs and meet and make new friends. Good sportsmanship and making sure that you and your dog have a good time are as or more important as winning.

Show-giving Organizations

While the AKC is the preeminent dog organization in the United States, there are other show-giving organizations. Bull Terriers are also recognized by the United Kennel Club, Rarities, and International All Breed Canine Association. Showing at all-around AKC shows means that all other breeds are showing at the same show

The most famous contemporary Bull Terrier, CH Rocky Tops Sundance Kid ROM (Rufus), won Silverwood, many specialties, many Best In Show, and Westminster.

golden brindles, and white for white dogs. Do not use purple or blue or other flashy colors. Professional handlers don't use them, so a gaudy lead tends to make the handler look amateurish, as does a lead that is too long.

✔ Wear comfortable shoes and a clean, attractive outfit with pockets. Easy access to pockets is important. Most dogs react to bait or toys or both. Having a small stash of their favorite snacks

and a special toy handy can help a handler get the attention and expression he wants.

Silverwood

In the late 1960s Hope and Bill Colket, leading American breeders, proposed the idea of a major Bull Terrier trophy show. Renowned English breeder Raymond Oppenheimer helped

to all observers. To the AKC, Silverwood is essentially a fun match. Many lose sight of that, but things usually go very well and the event is something of an ultimate experience for breed devotees. All true Bull Terrier people want to attend Silverwood at least once in their lives; having once attended, most return.

Judging by committee: For Bull Terrier folk, the unique Silverwood competition is the most significant event of the year. To compete, dogs must qualify by virtue of a Canadian or AKC Championship or other win under a breeder judge at a Recognition of Merit (ROM) show. It has been called judging by committee, since two judges judge each class. The morning competition is Colored Dogs, White Dogs, Colored Females, then White Females. Judges do not confer with each other at this point. Each can select up to four dogs in each category or more if the entry numbers permit. After lunch, finalists return to the ring and from each class the judges agree upon a winner and a reserve. If they do not agree, a third judge makes a referee decision between the two dogs in contention at that point. Finally four dogs, one from each class, come into the ring. The Silverwood winner is selected and the reserve from his or her class comes in to compete with the remaining three dogs. A reserve to the Silverwood winner is then selected, along with a Best of Opposite Sex and Best of Opposite Variety. This means that if a white dog won Silverwood, one of the coloreds must be selected for Best of Opposite Variety. Most consider Silverwood a breeder's showcase. It is an enjoyable opportunity to show and see other top-quality Bull Terriers, win *or* not.

further that effort and in 1970 the first such show was held. Sadly, by that time, both Hope and Bill had been killed in separate car accidents. The trophy competition was named to honor them and their Silverwood kennel. Silverwood was originally intended as less of a competition than as an opportunity to bring together leading breeders and top dogs to exchange ideas and information and to view excellent dogs. Over time, that tradition has largely been maintained in this elegant ballroom event. Showing at and watching Silverwood is classy and comfortable. It is also free

Breeder judges: Judges all weekend, except for performance, must be breeder judges. At all BTCA specialties only breeder judges can award ROM points. The ROM will be basically outlined/explained next. Generally, the preference for breeder judges stems from the long-held, possibly erroneous, belief that judges from other breeds are not particularly interested in the Bull Terrier and do not have an eye for them. The other critical element in the insistence on Breeder Judges has to do with the intense desire of Bull Terrier breeder/owners to work with and show their own dogs, rather than engage professional handlers. Around the world, Bull Terrier specialties are judged by breeder judges.

Other events: In coordination with the AKC, the BTCA offers the Bull Terrier National Specialty and other events a few days on either side of Silverwood. In addition to sweepstakes, the program includes futurity, agility, obedience, Therapy Dog International, Canine Good Citizen testing, and Junior Showmanship. Most feel that the Canine Good Citizen (CGC) title is so important, that the BTCA generously offers free testing at Silverwood. Judges' education and health seminars are also held. Sprinkled in are open and private cocktail parties, meetings, and, depending on the sponsoring club, a variety of side trips and programs.

Recognition of Merit and the Venues Where Awarded

Another unique aspect in showing Bull Terriers has to do with the Recognition of Merit (ROM), which is offered only at specified shows, spon-

sored or approved by the BTCA and judged by a Breeder Judge. In other breeds, ROM usually is the acronym for Reward of Merit and it usually is a reward at a show, not an affixed title.

Because of English complaints and a general feeling that American and Canadian championship titles were easier in comparison to English titles, the ROM system was instituted by the BTCA in 1978. It is an additional title for Bull Terriers only, and signifying a title that is roughly equivalent to an English championship. Bull Terrier owners are extremely proud of earning this title. For most, it means they have taken their dog(s) into the toughest competition and won.

Points: Usually, a ROM weekend consists of two to four shows. A three-point ROM is a

White Bull Terriers have tended to be given starring roles more often than their colored brethren.

Bull Terrier Clubs in the United States and Canada

BTC of Central Arizona	Barbary Coast BTC (CA)	Blue Ridge BTC (TN)
Buckeye BTC (OH)	BTC of Canada	BTC of Canada—Alberta
BTC of Canada-BC	Columbia River BTC	BT Confederacy of SE
BTC of Dallas	BT Fanciers Assn. (Canada)	Fort Dearborn BTC (IL)
BTC of Metro Detroit	Garden State BTC (NJ)	Golden State BTC (CA)
Golden Triangle BTC (PA)	BTC of Hawaii	Illiana BTC (IN)
Knickerbocker BTC (NY)	Mile High BTC (CO)	Monterey Bay BTC (CA)
BTC of New England (MA)	Central New Jersey BTC	BTC of Oklahoma City
Orange Coast BTC (AL)	BTC of Philadelphia	BTC of Puget Sound (WA)
BTC of St. Louis	BTC of Tampa Bay	Texas Gulf Coast BTC

Links to most of these clubs can be found at *BTCA.com*

major and is the most that can be earned at any one show. One- and two-point ROMs are also given and while not majors, contribute to the total 10 ROMs (to include 2 majors) required to award the ROM affix/title. It's a little complex and the rules occasionally change, but essentially, ROM points are based on the number of dogs defeated. ROM points are given in addition to and are unrelated to AKC points. ROM shows are throughout the United States and Canada. Most are in Eastern states, but in the past decade, clubs in the West have had an expanding influence and have been able to offer more opportunities to show and earn ROM points.

Location: Silverwood moves from place to place. Where the show will be held is determined about two or three years in advance, based largely on regional clubs bidding to host the show. Typically, Silverwood and most specialties tend to be held in the East and as in many other breeds, attendance and entries at East Coast venues tend to be higher than when those shows are held in the West.

Travel: Airline travel has become more difficult and fares to fly dogs have risen astronomically in the past few years. Soaring gas prices have inhibited both car and recreational vehicle travel. Still, most dedicated breeders and owners will somehow manage to attend Silverwood and regional specialties.

Value: Attendance at specialties and supported shows has rewards in terms of meeting old friends and making new ones. It also gives breeders a chance to assess dogs for breeding possibilities and puppies' potential, and to evaluate judges.

A Balanced Portfolio

Very little in life is more important than how we use our time—it tells us who we are and where we are going. Just as brokers advise that our finances should be balanced, so should we consider our investment in time with our Bullies. Conformation showing at both specialties and all-rounder shows can be challenging and exciting. Agility, obedience, rally, and therapy

The Canine Good Citizen title is achievable for every good-natured Bull Terrier.

training are also wonderful ways to enjoy life with a Bully. Most Bull Terriers can participate in all these activities, but an effort and a commitment of time and energy must be made. Since Canine Good Citizen represents common sense, and everyday good manners, all Bull Terriers should earn this title.

Most importantly, your Bull Terrier needs to be involved in your day-to-day life. Almost all Bull Terriers love traveling and are wonderful companions on vacations. Your Bull Terrier is a family member. She is the three-year-old in a dog suit that loves sharing activities, training, treats, hugs, and just about everything in between.

THOSE SPECIAL SENIORS

Healthy, well-cared-for Bull Terriers normally have life spans of approximately 10 to 14 years. Several of our Bull Terriers lived to 15 years and I've read about some who lived to be 16.

How Long Do They Live?

An important component of living long is that well-cared-for Bull Terriers tend to have extended quality of life in their golden years. Most in old age are actually quite spry and

Bull Terrier Age	Approximation to Human Age
5	40
6	45
7	50
8	55
9	60–61
10	66
11	72
12	77
13	82
14	88
15	93
16	99

their deaths often seem relatively sudden, with little warning. The old rule of thumb that one dog year is equivalent to seven human years is now considered inaccurate. Current thinking indicates that Bull Terriers enter senior status at approximately seven to eight years of age, and are considered to be getting elderly at about ten to eleven years. Some gray a bit around the muzzle, while others tend to remain young looking into really old age. Thanks to good genetics, loving care, and a quality diet, many Bull Terriers achieve senior status, but may be prone to some geriatric issues that need owner awareness and attention.

Geriatric Care

What owners must recognize is that Bull Terriers tend to be stoic and often bear aches and pain in silence. Especially if they are having a good time, Bull Terriers may show minimal

Seniors enjoy a relaxed pace, like having a little afternoon snooze on the porch.

signs of discomfort or illness. Often until a problem is critical, an owner may not recognize that a Bull Terrier is not doing well.

Seniors usually need moderate exercise, proper nutrition, comfortable rest, and companionship. They need quiet time with the family, and they may need a little help getting onto the couch. Seniors should have annual visits to their veterinarian, who will especially want to check teeth, eyes, and lungs, discuss diet and overall health, and do blood and urine work. Blood tests should include checks for thyroid function, which sometimes falters a bit in seniors. Kidney functions also need to be checked and protein creatinine (urine) tests are more accurate for this than blood tests are. Caring veterinarians will call and discuss results with owners.

Hearing: Owners may note signs of less acute hearing. A veterinarian will want to verify that a problem may not be due to an infection or foreign object, but some reduction of hearing is normal in older Bull Terriers. Most dogs easily learn hand signals in doing basic obedience. These hand signals can effectively assist communication, if hearing diminishes.

Pace and reactions: Owners may also note a slowing of pace and reactions. Owners may see some stiffness in movement, especially in cold or damp weather, in getting up and down stairs, or getting up from a nap.

Diet: Veterinarians and natural health care personnel may suggest adding fatty acids to the diet. While Omega 6 fatty acids are an essential nutrient and important to the maintenance of healthy skin, Omega 6 can also aggravate inflammatory responses in some dogs. Of more use may be Omega 3 fatty acids, which are believed to be important to brain development in young animals and can help dogs suffering from allergies, arthritis, and some kidney diseases. Omega 3 is usually in capsule form, combined with B and E vitamins, which help the fatty acids work more effectively. Owners should also ask their veterinarians about giving glucosamine and chondroitin, which seem to help human and canine joints and cartilage with considerable safety.

Drugs: A veterinarian may also recommend drugs such as Rimadyl for arthritis. Prior to any long-term administration of a medication like this nonsteroid anti-inflammatory drug (NSAID), veterinarians will want to test for kidney and liver functions, carefully review the Bull Terrier's health history, and know about any other medications being given. Owners should ask to discuss all drugs being prescribed, possible short-term side effects, possible interactions, and subsequent requirements for testing for any long-term effects. Owners should ask for written details on risks affiliated with any medication that is going to be administered.

Injury or muscle atrophy: Other possibilities for a Bull Terrier slowing down include injury or muscle atrophy. Some atrophy can be prevented by regular, mild exercise, while some may be related to degenerative diseases, such as Cushings. These diseases are fortunately not well known in Bull Terriers.

Vision: Aging eyes often appear hazy or cloudy or have a bluish cast, which are relatively normal conditions. These do not seem to seriously affect vision. Vision is affected by cataracts, which seem to give the eyes a whitish, opaque look. Veterinarians can determine if an actual problem exists and will discuss potential remedies.

Canine senility: Elderly Bull Terriers occasionally exhibit signs of something similar to canine senility. As a dog ages, his brain seems less capable as neurotransmitters function more slowly. Cognitive Dysfunction Syndrome or CDS should

Life slows down, but love remains real!

be suspected when a dog seems disoriented, doesn't respond to his name or basic commands, forgets routines, stares into space, paces or appears lost and confused, becomes incontinent, shuns affection, and/or becomes agitated for no obvious reason. Keeping an older dog mentally active can help stimulate his senses and improve his mental and physical health. Real personality changes require a checkup and discussion with the family veterinarian.

Senior Needs

Seniors often do *not* need annual vaccines other than those required by state regulation such as rabies, and this should be discussed with the veterinarian. However, seniors often do need extra bedding, softer blankets, and protection from drafts and cold weather. Therapeutic beds can help relieve aches at pressure points. Seniors love attention and are delighted with gentle

Senior Bull Terriers, just like puppies, are great treasures!

brushing and an occasional warm bath with a mild shampoo. Those who understand and enjoy the benefits of aromatherapy may wish to include their Bull Terrier by keeping him nearby during sessions. Bull Terriers absolutely love being massaged and it is great therapy for them. Techniques vary, but temperate massage can stimulate circulation, soothe aches, and genuinely give comfort, while offering the owner a chance to share some quality relaxation. In addition to the continuing closeness, it is an opportunity to examine the Bull Terrier for lumps and bumps.

Rescues: Occasionally, rescue centers encounter the turn-in of elderly, well-behaved Bull Terriers. People often seem to feel that if something or someone is old, he is no longer useful or of interest. Nothing could be further from the truth. Being older does not mean that a Bull Terrier is any less sweet or funny or personable. Seniors adore their family and each other. They occasion-

ally quibble, but mostly they show each other respect, grooming each other and vying for positions on the couch. Seniors are a special source of delight. While they are not as quick as they used to be, senior Bull Terriers are still resourceful and clever. They are magnificent company.

It's Time to Say Good-bye

At some point, an owner may have to deal with assessing whether quality of life has been so lost that continuation of life is not justifiable. Bull Terriers tend to suffer in silence, giving few clues to internal pain. By the time most owners recognize the depth of a problem, it is very likely that it is time or even past time to seriously consider letting go. When our loved ones are unable to enjoy normal activities, such as eating, walking, or living with dignity, it is time. When they are suffering from consistent pain or persistent diarrhea and vomiting, it is time and perhaps past time.

Decisions about health, quality of life, and death are personal and individual, but consultation with the family veterinarian can help provide information on options and perhaps help with additional understanding about the pet's condition, prospects, and the role of humane euthanasia in alleviating interminable pain. Many veterinarians make house visits, so that the beloved pet can relax in the surroundings that are the most familiar and comfortable. A Bull Terrier will be soothed by the calm and reassuring presence of those who have loved and shared his life and now courageously share in his departure from this time and place. Owners should be comforted by the ease with which their much-loved Bull Terrier passes from life into peaceful rest.

Parents will want to help children deal with their Bull Terrier's decline and death. Fortunately, children are often more perceptive and flexible than we realize. I was once told about the relative calmness of a youngster observing the euthanasia of an adored pet. When asked how he managed to deal so well with the short life of his dog, he responded, "Mom told me that we come to earth to learn how to love and take care of each other. Dogs learn that quickly, so I figure they don't have to stay as long."

While most of us feel a dreadful, soul wrenching loss when one of our Bull Terriers dies, anyone who suffers acutely for any length of time should seek professional counseling. Our relationships with our Bull Terriers are very special. Their lives are about joy. They want their families to enjoy their lives too!

Bull Terriers help us rediscover the simple joys and truths in life.

Parting Thoughts

Theo Marples in his book *Show Dogs* summarized the section on Bull Terriers with these words: "The Bull-terrier holds a very high position amongst the Terrier varieties by reason of its sterling worth as a companion and as a dog. He has no superior in the matter of pluck, gameness and indomitable courage, of which virtues he may be said to be the very embodiment, while as a companion, he is as harmless as a kitten, as docile and tractable as a child and as staunch and true as steel."

For most of us, the joy of Bull Terrier companionship has much to do with rediscovery of simple pleasures such as watching butterflies, napping on a warm afternoon, playing ball, watching television, catching popcorn, and finding fun in almost everything. The simplicity of sharing time together on a walk or sitting quietly on the back step, or watching the incredible antics of these mischievous childlike dogs bring us back to a recognition that real happiness is found in the heart and home. And the happiest homes are those that have a Bull Terrier member of the family!

Organizations

American Kennel Club
51 Madison Avenue
New York, NY 10038
(212) 696-8200
www.akc.org

For registration information:
American Kennel Club
5580 Centerview Drive
Raleigh, NC 27606
(919) 233-9767

Marin County Humane Society
http://www.marin-humane.org
(of interest for their excellent socialization and
training programs)

National Kennel Club
255 Indian Ridge Road
P.O. Box 331
Blaine, Tennessee 37709
www.nationalkennelclub.com

United Kennel Club
100 East Kilgore Road
Kalamazoo, MI 49001-5598
616-343-9020
www.ukcdogs.com

Health Committee

Bull Terrier Club of America Health Committee
*http://www.btca.com/Cooke%20Content%20Pages/
   HEALTH.htm*

Rescue

Bull Terrier Club of America Rescue
http://btca.com/rescue/index.html

Periodicals

Barks
Victoria Corse
P.O. Box 995
Marshfield, MA 02050-0995
http://btca.com/Publications/btcapub.html

BTCA Record
Naomi Waynee
1122 E. Carol Avenue
Phoenix, AZ 85020-2611
http://btca.com/Publications/record.html

Just Terriers
P.O. Box 518
Trappe, MD 21673
http://www.justterriers.com

Books

Drewes, Marilyn. *All About the Bull Terriers and
   Miniature Bull Terriers.* Colorado: Alpine Blue
   Ribbon Books, 2005.
Fogle, Bruce. *First Aid for Dogs.* New York:
   Penguin, 1997.
McConnell, Patricia B. *How to Be the Leader
   of the Pack... And Have Your Dog Love
   You for It.* Wisconsin: Dog's Best Friend,
   1996.
Millan, Cesar and Melissa Jo Peltier. *Cesar's
   Way.* New York: Random House; Harmony,
   2006.
The Monks of New Skete. *The Art of Raising a
   Puppy.* New York: Little, Brown, 1991.
———. *How to Be Your Dog's Best Friend.* New
   York: Little, Brown, 2002.
Palika, Liz. *Purebred Rescue Dog Adoption.*
   New Jersey: Wiley; Howell Book House,
   2004.

Prevention Health Books. *The Doctors Book of Home Remedies for Dogs and Cats.* New York: Bantam, 1997.

Siegal, Mordecai. *UC Davis Book of Dogs: The Complete Medical Reference Guide for Dogs and Puppies.* New York: HarperCollins, 1995.

Simon, John M. and Stephanie Pederson. *What Your Dog Is Trying to Tell You.* New York: St. Martin's, 2000.

Videos

AKC Breed Standard Videos
www.akc.org/store/

Sirius Puppy Training
www.siriuspup.com/

Puppies ready to take on the world, or a nap, whichever comes first.

Web Pages

Bull Terrier Club of America
http://btca.com/

International All Breed Canine Association of America
http://www.internationaldogshow.com/

Rarities Inc. (rare and AKC breeds)
http://www.raritiesinc.ca/

Sirius Dog Training
http://www.siriuspup.co

INDEX

About the Author

Carolyn and her husband David have been breeding and exhibiting Bull Terriers for over 25 years. The limited Brigadoon breeding program has produced a series of American and Canadian Champions, including multiple national specialty winners, ROM Champions, and group placing dogs. Currently the Bull Terrier columnist for the *AKC Gazette,* she has also been the Monterey Bay BTC Newsletter Editor for over 15 years and has contributed articles to several annuals and national magazines, including the Bull Terrier magazine *Barks, Just Terriers,* and *Dog News.*

Acknowledgments

I can't imagine life without a Bull Terrier, or three. While other breeds are wonderful, few are as personable and naturally childlike. I would like to thank my husband, David, for his wonderful help in reviewing text and slides, and for his consistent and generous support of my career over the years. I would like to thank the many wonderful Bull Terrier friends, especially our co-owners, who over the years have been caring, helpful, encouraging, and instructive. My thanks also to Anne McNamara and Seymour Weiss for their assistance in preparing this book for publication.

My biggest thanks would be to the wonderful Bull Terriers with whom we've been privileged to share our lives. We've learned so much from our four-legged companions.

Important Note

This pet owner's manual tells the reader how to buy or adopt, and care for, a Bull Terrier. The author and publisher consider it important to point out that the advice given in the book is meant primarily for normally developed dogs of excellent physical health and sound temperament.

Anyone who acquires a fully-grown dog should be aware that the animal has already formed its basic impressions of human beings. The new owner should observe the animal carefully, including its behavior toward humans, and, whenever possible, should meet the previous owner.

Caution is further advised in the association of children with dogs, and in meeting with other dogs, and in exercising the dog without a leash.

Even well-behaved and carefully supervised dogs can sometimes damage property or cause accidents. It is therefore in the owner's interest to be adequately insured against such eventualities, and we strongly urge all dog owners to purchase a liability policy that also covers their dog.

Photo Credits

Norvia Behling: 12, 14, 17, 36, 38, 55, 65, 66, 86, and 90; Kent Dannen: 2–3, 6, 13, 18, 22, 29, 34, 47, 52, 53, 63, 67, 69, 70, 71, 75, 76 (bottom left), 80, 87, 88, and 89; Tara Darling: 4, 5, 7, 19, 21, 23, 27, 37, 39, 41, 43, 56, 76 (top left), 77, and 81; Isabel Francais: 8, 9, 10, 11, 15, 16 (top right and left), 24, 25, 26, 31, 33, 35, 40, 44, 46, 48, 49, 54, 59, 60, 64, 68, 74, 78, 79, 82, 83, 85, 91, and 93.

Cover Photos

Tara Darling: front cover; Isabelle Francais: inside front cover; Norvia Behling: back cover and inside back cover.

All inquiries should be addressed to:
Barron's Educational Series, Inc.
250 Wireless Boulevard
Hauppauge, NY 11788
www.barronseduc.com

ISBN-13: 978-0-7641-3528-6
ISBN-10: 0-7641-3528-7

Library of Congress Catalog Card No. 2006013677

Library of Congress Cataloging-in-Publication Data
Alexander, Carolyn, 1943–
    Bull terriers : everything about purchase, care, nutrition, behavior, and training / Carolyn Alexander ; illustrations by Michele Earle-Bridges.
        p. (large print) cm. — (A complete pet owner's manual)
    Includes bibliographical references and index.
    ISBN-13: 978-0-7641-3528-6 (alk. paper)
    ISBN-10: 0-7641-3528-7 (alk. paper)
    1. Bull terrier. I. Title.

SF429.B8A44   2006
636.755'9—dc22   2006013677

Printed in China
9 8 7 6 5 4